THE ART OF INVESTIGATIVE INTERVIEWING

A Human Approach to Testimonial Evidence

Charles L. Yeschke

Butterworth-Heinemann
Boston   Oxford   Johannesburg   Melbourne   New Delhi   Singapore

∞ Recognizing the importance of preserving what has been written, Butterworth-Heinemann prints its books on acid-free paper whenever possible.

Butterworth-Heinemann supports the efforts of American Forests and the Global ReLeaf program in its campaign for the betterment of trees, forests, and our environment.

Library of Congress Cataloging-in-Publication Data

Yeschke, Charles L.
    The art of investigative interviewing : a human approach to
testimonial evidence / Charles L. Yeschke.
      p.   cm.
    Includes bibliographical references and index.
    ISBN 0-7506-9808-X (alk. paper)
    1. Interviewing in law enforcement. 2. Police questioning.
  I. Title.
  HV8073.Y475   1996
  363.2'54—dc20   96-19260
                                            CIP

British Library Cataloguing-in-Publication Data
A catalogue record for this book is available from the British Library.

The publisher offers special discounts on bulk orders of this book.
For information, please contact:
Manager of Special Sales
Butterworth-Heinemann
313 Washington Street
Newton, MA 02158-1626
Tel: 617-928-2500
Fax: 617-928-2620

For information on all Security publications available, contact our World Wide Web home page at: http://www.bh.com/sec

10 9 8 7 6 5 4 3 2

Printed in the United States of America

Contents

Mission Statement

It is my personal goal to encourage each state to mandate and fund specific training for law enforcement officers in the dynamics of human communication as they relate to the collection and preservation of testimonial evidence.

Introduction

This book was written for anyone who is involved, in any way, in investigative interviewing. It is intended to be useful to all levels of our judicial system, from patrol officers to judges, and from police recruits to twenty-year veterans. I hope it will be used not only in recruit training, but also in advanced in-service instruction, since all ranks can profit from better investigative techniques. In addition, this text can be used by paralegals, corporate security/loss prevention professionals, and private investigators—essentially anyone seeking a better way to gain testimonial evidence. With a comprehensive knowledge of interviewing techniques aimed at collecting solid testimonial evidence, police officers and other investigators can better serve and protect their communities.

The late John E. Reid showed me how to see my responsibilities as an investigator more clearly, and how to uncover the truth without using coercion. I used his affective interviewing techniques on the job with both the Central Intelligence Agency (CIA) and the Federal Bureau of Investigation (FBI). In hundreds of cases and thousands of interviews, I have used the process outlined in this text to pick out the guilty party. I wrote this book with four objectives: 1) to promote affective interviewing, 2) to encourage the law enforcement community to add course work in interviewing to police officer training, 3) to counteract the outdated, and often illegal, coercive tactics of the past, and 4) to further an ethical professionalism in our investigators.

POLICE OFFICER TRAINING
The Role of Patrol Officers

Because of a likely relationship between patrol time and crime prevention, communities want police officers on patrol. Patrol officers are expected to function as guardians, serving and protecting the public. While this approach is no doubt effective, crime is also prevented by the swift and certain apprehension of criminals. That apprehension requires the collection of evidence. If patrol officers are to complete even preliminary inquiries, they need sufficient time to interview victims, witnesses, and suspects. Too often, patrol officers are either forced to hurry to another call, or are ordered back on patrol before they have been able to handle a call thoroughly. In fact, patrol officers are frequently criticized by their superiors for spending too much time at a call. In many police agencies, even the incident report form reveals the official attitude; most provide only five or six lines at the bottom of the page, suggesting a desire for minimal detail. And yet, patrol officers in thousands of communities handle investigations from start to finish: they are the first officers on the scene of a crime and they present all police evidence in court.

A review of officer log/activity sheets shows that even when time is available, officers do not always conduct comprehensive interviews. Either they see interviewing as unimportant, their supervisors discourage it, or they are ill-equipped to handle the exchange during effective interviewing. Police officers often discover during court testimony that they should have interviewed more and better—but by then it is too late. Effective officers recognize that the patrol function requires as much skill and art as it does police science. The key element of any inquiry is the investigator's ability to interact with people and discover the truth. This text will help you develop that key element.

Current Basic Training

Only a few four-year criminal justice programs currently offer a separate course on interviewing. It is generally taught as part of a course on criminal investigation. Courses focusing solely on interviewing are found in some two-year community college programs in criminal justice or law enforcement. As a practical matter, police academies concentrate the training of police recruits on topics that the state believes will prepare them to serve and protect the community. The need to cover legally mandated topics within a certain amount of time, and with a limited amount of funding, restricts the training to about 330 hours. This amount of time is generally considered quite adequate, but the important topic of interviewing is ignored. In the typical training outlined in the nearby box, there is no mention of interviewing, interrogating, human interaction, or any aural communication skills.

And yet, testimonial evidence obtained through investigative interviewing accounts for about 80 percent of all evidence presented in court. In a criminal investigation, the truth is rarely obvious enough to be determined by superficial methods. The truth is uncovered by an investigator following a diagnostic method of collecting and examining evidence—including testimonial evidence. The investigator's diagnosis follows a close analysis of facts and interviewee behavior patterns that support or deny a working hypothesis about the guilt or innocence of an interviewee. Academies regard the teaching of interviewing techniques to recruits as too expensive, and assume that officers will learn them indirectly while studying other topics. But we are no more born with the skills to collect testimonial evidence than we are born with the innate ability to handle firearms properly or provide first aid. Patrol officers must learn how to interact with other human beings in a professional manner, just as they must learn when it is appropriate to use deadly force. With this in mind, current patrol officer training falls short and carries a long-term consequence. Police officers often wait years before they qualify for special training in interpersonal communication and interviewing skills. In the meantime, they have learned techniques, which may or may not be effective, the hard way—on the street. By the time they qualify to attend specialized seminars on interviewing, many officers have missed several opportunities to solve important crimes. I am convinced that many officers are unsuccessful in law enforcement because they were never properly trained in the techniques of interviewing. They could better serve society if they were taught interviewing skills at the beginning of their careers and given refresher courses periodically. This text intends to teach those skills.

TYPICAL BASIC TRAINING FOR PATROL OFFICERS

Hours	Course/Activity	Hours	Course/Activity
1	Critical Decision Making (Hands-On)	2	Chemical Munitions
		2	Ethics
		2	Fraud & Forgery
1	Death Investigation	2	Gangs
1	Defensive Tactics Orientation (Classroom)	2	Initial Meeting with Supervisors and Equipment Issue
1	Report Writing		
1	Orientation	2	Police Pursuits
2	9 mm Qualification (Daytime)	2	Shotgun Familiarization (Classroom)
2	Bias Crimes		

Hours	*Course/Activity*	*Hours*	*Course/Activity*
2	Shotgun Qualification (Daytime)	3	Search and Seizure Practice
2	Use of Deadly Force	3	Sexual Assault Practice
2	Vice	3	Weapon Retention (Hands-On)
2	Victim/Witness Rights	4	9 mm Qualification (Nighttime)
2	Vulnerable Adults		
3	Accident Scene Management (Practice)	4	9 mm Familiarization (Classroom)
3	Assault/Burglary, Robbery/Burglary, Theft	4	Bombs and Hazardous Materials
3	Auto Theft	4	Booking and Fingerprinting (Hands-On)
3	Crime Investigation Practice	4	Child Abuse
3	Crime Investigation Techniques (Generic)	4	Constitutional Law Review
3	Crime Investigation Techniques to Include: Assault, Crime Scene, and Review	4	Felony Stop Lecture (Classroom)
		4	Fundamentals: Shooting and Range Rules
3	Critical Decision Making	4	In-Progress Crimes (Classroom)
3	D.U.I. (Practice)	4	Misdemeanor Traffic Stops (Classroom)
3	Juvenile Issues		
3	Latent and Inked Fingerprints (Classroom)	4	Narcotics
		4	Prisoner Transport (Hands-On)
3	Patrol Functions		
3	Pedestrian Stops (Classroom)	4	Revolver Familiarization (Hands-On at Range)
3	Pedestrian Stops (Hands-On)		
3	Radio Procedures and Information Systems	4	Sexual Assault (Classroom)

(continued)

Hours	Course/Activity	Hours	Course/Activity
5	Dynamic Techniques (Hands-On)	10	Felony Stop Practice
6	Crisis Intervention Practice	12	Traffic Law
7	Crisis Intervention (Includes 1 Hour Ho??)	13	Misdemeanor Traffic Stop Practice (Classroom) (9 H??)
7	D.U.I. (Classroom)	16	9 mm Training (Hands-On at Range)
7	Radar		
8	Accident Scene Management (Classroom)	16	Driving School
		18	In-Progress Crimes Practice
8	Evidence (Classroom)	20	Dual Baton (Hands-On)
8	Searching and Handcuffing (Hands-On)	22	Unarmed Defensive Tactics (Hands-On)
8	Shotgun (Hands-On at Range)		

ETHICS FOR LAW ENFORCEMENT PROFESSIONALS

The Foundation of Ethics

Despite all the guidelines, the laws, the shining examples, and the taboos, we all reach a stage when we must look to ourselves and decide what we believe and where we stand. Judged by our deeds, we must take responsibility for our acts. In 1842, the poet Alfred Lord Tennyson asked, "Ah! when shall all men's good be each man's rule?" For "all men's good" to be "each man's rule," we must act with reason, for, as human beings, reason is our unique advantage. Ethics belong to the inner voice, the source of self-control. According to former Supreme Court Justice Potter Stewart, "Ethics is defined as knowing the difference between what you have a right to do and what is the right thing to do." Because this text relates interviewer behavior to success during investigations, how the investigator treats the interviewee will, to large extent, determine the outcome of the interview. Because the outcome can demolish another person's life and injure society, the investigator's behavior must be ethical. In their article "Doing the Right Thing," H.B. Karp and Bob Abramms discuss ethics which apply not only to life in general, but which, I believe, particularly apply to investigative interviewing:

- Values define who you are. All ethical decisions are determined by values that are clear and uncompromising statements about what is critically important. In organizations, clear values drive mission statements, strategic plans, and effective, results-oriented behavior.
- Having a code of ethics supports the concept of dignity as the central factor that drives human interaction in the workplace. Most organizational codes of ethics clearly call for behaviors that demand that people treat each other with respect.
- A code of ethics provides a commonly held set of guidelines that will provide a consistent, value-driven basis for judging what is right or wrong in any given situation and which establishes the outer limits of acceptable behavior.
- Only actions are judged to be ethical or unethical. Ethics do not define what is acceptable about an action, as much as they define what is not acceptable.
- If a new code of ethics is truly going to be operational, people have to have an opportunity to see where the ethics originate, what purposes they serve, and how they relate to each individual.

- The only ethics that are realistic and worth supporting are situational ethics. That is, the ongoing circumstances of a given situation determine which subsequent actions will be effective, appropriate, and ethical.

THE CALIFORNIA PEACE OFFICERS' ASSOCIATION'S "CODE OF PROFESSIONAL CONDUCT AND RESPONSIBILITIES FOR PEACE OFFICERS."

In its nine canons, this code enumerates the ethical standards of professional conduct expected of police officers in their relationships with the public, the criminal justice system, and the profession. The canons are offered here as an excellent example of a professional law enforcement code of ethics.

The Canons of Ethics

1. Peace Officers shall uphold the Constitution of the United States, the State Constitution, and all laws enacted or established pursuant to legally constituted authority.
2. Peace Officers shall be aware of and shall use proper and ethical procedures in discharging their official duties and responsibilities.
3. Peace Officers shall regard the discharge of their duties as a public trust and shall recognize their responsibilities to the people whom they are sworn to protect and serve.
4. Peace Officers will so conduct their public and private life that they exemplify the high standards of integrity, trust, and morality demanded of a member of the peace officer profession.

5. Peace Officers shall recognize that our society holds the freedom of the individual as a paramount precept which shall not be infringed upon without just, legal, and necessary cause.
6. Peace Officers shall assist in maintaining the integrity and competence of the peace officer profession.
7. Peace Officers shall cooperate with other officials and organizations who are using legal and ethical means to achieve the goals and objectives of the peace officer profession.
8. Peace Officers shall not compromise their integrity, nor that of their agency or profession, by accepting, giving, or soliciting any gratuity.
9. Peace Officers shall observe the confidentiality of information available to them through any source, as it relates to the peace officer profession.

Adopting a Code of Ethics

Law enforcement professionals possess the awesome responsibility to affect the life, liberty, and happiness of the individuals within their jurisdiction. This responsibility refers specifically to the proper use of power and authority. If we are to expect investigators to behave in positive ways, they should receive training which will support ethical behavior. While most states have set certain standards for law enforcement training and education, they have not set ethical standards for conduct. At this writing, only a few states have formulated codes of ethical conduct (see nearby box for those set in the state of California). Basic ethical principles for law enforcement professionals should be required in all states to fortify the standards established by state laws.

Principle Objective

Although law enforcement professionals, like those in medicine and law, are regulated by laws that buttress society's confidence in reliable, competent service, legislation has never set sophisticated standards governing the ethical behavior of professionals. Professional codes of ethics do. Without their ethical codes, the legal and medical professions would not retain their high status in our society. Each profession must take the initiative to adopt a code of ethics that is particular to the specific services it renders to society. Policies and procedures are the vehicles that an organization uses to communicate its ethical expectations and requirements to its employees. These guidelines provide an effective supplement to individual judgment.

The principal objective of ethical law enforcement professionals is to render service to society with full respect for the dignity of all in the determination of the truth. Confidence in the professional law enforcement officer is created through a public acknowledgment of the officer's integrity, education, and experience. Officers should observe all statutes of society, uphold the dignity and honor of the profession, and accept its self-imposed disciplines. Officers should expose, without hesitation, the illegal or unethical conduct of fellow members of the profession. The law enforcement profession should safeguard the public and itself against officers who are deficient in moral character or professional competence by pledging itself to identify and eliminate any unqualified persons from its ranks. Above all, law enforcement professionals must dedicate themselves to fostering and maintaining the highest ethical standards and principles of practice.

ETHICAL INTERVIEWING
Professional Integrity

The public must have confidence in the law enforcement professional's integrity and professional standards. Law enforcement professionals must not jeopardize their integrity by personal, political, or financial associations that would improperly influence a criminal investigation. The law enforcement professional's report should be a clear, concise summary of what occurred during the investigation and record all pertinent information. Criminal investigations must be conducted in a professional atmosphere in which no one tampers with evidence, and no one physically or psychologically compels an innocent person to confess. We must be preoccupied not just with what we do, but with how we do it. I consider the following list of behaviors unethical:

- Using interrogation tactics instead of interviewing tactics
- Treating each interviewee as though culpable, with little or no regard for the destructive public relations and psychological damage inflicted on interviewees who are blameless
- Making threats
- Making illegal promises
- Using coercion
- Using duress
- Using force or the threat of force
- Employing ruthless methods
- Falsely imprisoning the interviewee
- Demeaning and insulting the interviewee
- Ignoring the interviewee's dignity

These and similar tactics have been used in the past in interviews with victims and witnesses as well as suspects. It is time for change. In the following box I offer a sample code of ethics for effective interviewing. Throughout this text I recommend tactics and techniques specifically chosen to promote the willing cooperation of interviewees to reveal the truth. Reputable law enforcement professionals cannot claim to be perfect—they are, after all, human—but they can hold themselves to ethical guidelines. It is time that those involved in investigative interviewing be specifically taught to distinguish between ethical and unethical, legal and illegal, interviewing techniques. With comprehensive training, we can encourage all levels of law enforcement to use more finesse and less force!

A SAMPLE CODE OF ETHICS FOR EFFECTIVE INTERVIEWING

- To verify the truth fairly, impartially, and objectively
- To make no false statements and claims regarding personal qualifications
- To maintain the highest standards of moral, ethical, and professional conduct
- To be governed by laws of equity and justice in the performance of all duties
- To respect the inherent dignity of all people
- To be just, fair, and impartial with each individual, irrespective of social, political, racial, ethnic, or religious group, economic status, or physical characteristics
- To discharge professional duties and obligations with independence, dignity, and self-respect
- To keep all decisions and reports scrupulously free of any personal, financial, political, fraternal, social, or improper influence
- To refrain from false or misleading reporting
- To accept no illegal or improper remuneration for services rendered
- To refrain from representing competing or conflicting interests when such representation is, or gives the appearance of being, unethical
- To refrain from slanderous or libelous public criticism of the law enforcement profession or its membership, by recognizing that the welfare and advancement of the profession and society supersede personal desires and ambitions

- To recommend and accept for membership in the profession those who strive in every way to be a credit to the profession
- To support the purposes and objectives of the law enforcement profession

REFERENCES

Karp, H.B., and Bob Abramms. "Doing the Right Thing." *Training and Development* (August 1992), 37–41.

Yeschke, Charles L. *Interviewing: A Forensic Guide to Interrogation,* 2nd ed. Charles C. Thomas. Springfield, IL 1993.

Human Needs and Deception in the Interview

EVIDENCE AND THE AFFECTIVE INTERVIEW

In general, investigators uncover the most useful evidence by interviewing the victims of a crime, any witnesses, and the suspects in that crime. As investigators sort through a mass of detail, it is the interview which, potentially, can illuminate guilt. The affective interview takes into account, and makes primary, the emotions and feelings of the interviewee. On the other side of the interview table, the affective interview encourages the interviewer to behave with sensitivity and perception. Combining the two points of view produces an interview that is more about the process of human interaction than it is about the end product. Nevertheless, by emphasizing the process, the affective interview better produces the successful outcome—truthful information.

Investigators proficient in the affective interview know when to talk and when to listen. By understanding the degree to which the interviewer's behavior directly influences the interviewee's, the investigator comes prepared to approach each exchange with positive expectations, acceptance, patience, and persistence. In addition, the investigator comes to the interview better equipped to recognize an interviewee's deception and, consequently, uncovers the truth.

Success in influencing the behavior of interviewees—in convincing them to answer questions honestly—begins with your attempt to understand the causes of their behavior. I believe that crimes are committed to satisfy the basic interpersonal needs of control, belonging, and intimacy. In one form or another, these three often lie at the core of the criminal personality. Underneath differences of culture, "Humans are all equipped with the same emotional repertoire, the same basic needs, the same basic defenses" (Bennis et al., p. 93). If the interviewer understands that he or she shares the same needs as the person being questioned, then the investigator can use this understanding to establish rapport and search for the truth. The effective (and affective) interviewer sets the stage for eliciting accurate information by knowing and accepting the emotional needs that motivate all human activity.

Universal Human Needs

In his classic work *Motivation and Personality*, the eminent American psychologist Abraham Maslow identified six levels of motivation, all of which underlie behavior and reflect attempts to satisfy universal human needs. People are motivated to pursue:

- Physiological stability (sufficient food, water, and oxygen)
- Safety and security
- Love and belonging
- Esteem, competence, and prestige

- Self-actualization (to become what one is capable of becoming)
- Knowledge that satisfies curiosity

As the psychiatrist William Menninger states, "The problem is one of achieving a balance between what we want and what we get. We all want things, but the more adult among us learn to master our frustrations and to recognize that we cannot have what we want when we want it. To be truly adult and efficient persons, we have to learn to find satisfaction in daily life" (Menninger, pp. 22-28). Thus, we ingeniously modify our behavior to adapt to barriers in order to resolve the complicated, muddled messes we may find ourselves in. We either define and overcome the obstacles that are blocking the satisfaction of our needs, or become frustrated at our failure. Any one of Maslow's needs may motivate not only the execution of a crime, but how the main participants will respond during questioning. I believe that unless some basic participant needs are satisfied, interviews tend to be little more than a waste of time. It is not that it is impossible to obtain information without fulfilling those needs, it is just that the more needs the interviewer fulfills, the more likely it is that investigative information will be forthcoming and accurate. The anticipation and satisfaction of needs is central to affective interviewing. Let's look at how some of these needs influence the scope of an interview.

Safety and Security

An individual needs to feel physically safe in his home, his neighborhood, and, for our purposes, in an interview. We try to satisfy our needs by maintaining physical comfort and avoiding the unsafe. This primary need for security becomes particularly important in an interview. If you fail to anticipate this need, tension will develop and last as long as you lack such understanding. If an investigator is a badge-pushing, bone-crusher type, the interviewee senses a misuse of power and probably will refuse to cooperate.

Be careful when aroused to anger. Even though you have been trained to use deadly force, it is not appropriate to display or hint at that training. When investigative matters become intense and distressful enough to provoke emotional involvement, proficient interviewers desensitize and detach.

Because the United States is a diverse nation of many cultures, inevitably, you will come in contact with people who exhibit values different from your own. Cultural values are social rules or accepted routes that people follow toward fulfilling needs. The foods people eat are obvious manifestations of cultural values; others are more subtle and complex. Because the interviewee needs to feel safe, the investigator cannot impose his or her values by punishing, either verbally or physically, interviewees who exhibit different cultural preferences (Bennis). We all acknowledge that, while we may not like particular foods, the fact that people eat them doesn't make them wrong. Likewise, the fact that someone acts differently than you do, does not necessarily make this action wrong. The person may be following behavioral norms learned as part of his or her cultural heritage. As long as what people do is not illegal, you are wise to accept their behavior without bias.

In order to promote our sense of safety and security, we seek to control our environments by maintaining satisfactory relationships with other people. Clearly, the interviewer seeks to control the interview by adopting the proactive role and asking questions. On the surface, the interviewer has the power. But the interviewee may not necessarily submit and relinquish control until he or she feels it is safe to do so. The interviewee reacts against power and control either by trying to establish an equal footing with the interviewer through cooperation, or by exercising his power not to cooperate. The interviewee tries to establish his own dominance by refusing to divulge information. If the interviewer understands this struggle for control over the interview environment, he or she can modify behavior to promote cooperation.

Loving and Belonging

Human beings are social animals with interpersonal needs. We do things together and interact with each other. We need to feel that we belong to groups and we seek esteem from the people in those groups. In all of our interpersonal relationships, there is a degree to which we like or dislike the other person, and a degree to which we dominate or submit. We express our liking or our desire to dominate through conversation—we talk to each other. Conversation answers the need to feel that we belong. The bowling team, biking group, writers club, and other such gatherings all promote a sense of belonging and intimacy. An individual joins these groups not only to do things he or she enjoys, but to take advantage of the opportunity for fulfillment through conversation. When interviewees believe that they are choosing to share information, conversing, not just submitting to the other's power by answering questions, the investigator receives the pay-off. Through conversation the skillful interviewer guides the way toward the desired goal, a revelation of the truth.

Self-Actualization and Esteem

It has been said that man's greatest fear is not of dying, but of feeling unfit to live. The self is a composite of what one feels, believes, wants, and worries about. Out of these subjective characteristics one constructs a self-image, and thinks of oneself as unique, with an inner self vastly different from the rest of humanity. The individual treasures his or her sense of self, and is frequently reluctant to reveal inner thoughts. Backed by an overriding motivation to do whatever is necessary to defend a self-image, an interviewee protects and enhances it with every action.

Self-esteem, closely tied to self-image, is worth to self and encompasses the need for achievement, mastery, dignity, independence, and freedom. Maintaining self-esteem, or "saving face," is central to interview participants. It is important to empathize with their attitudes and the roles they play in order to protect their self-esteem. If they feel that cooperation carries the high price of low self-esteem, they will not cooperate.

Esteem, on the other hand, consists of worth in the eyes of others—colleagues, peers, subordinates, and superiors. It is tied not only to the position one occupies, but more particularly, to the personal qualities of expertise, contribution, and warmth. Most people maintain the illusion that they are independent, reasonable, and competent human beings making sensible assumptions and conclusions. But our feelings are like nerve ends, sensors searching for public acceptance, and some people struggle desperately to achieve this approval. Those succumbing to temptation may feel the heavy weight of disapproval when they violate society's standards. When dealing with suspects, avoid the role of social judge and refrain from speaking out against repellent acts of omission or commission. If you can hide your distaste and help the interviewee believe that his or her behavior (the manifestation of the inner self) is acceptable, the person becomes more willing to provide information. If you wish to ensure a successful interview, try not to make the interviewees appear foolish. Actively listen to what interviewees have to say by exhibiting understanding and acceptance. Help interviewees strive for self-expression and self-fulfillment.

By the same token, be secure in your own identity. Understand yourself, and maintain a sturdy philosophical core. To promote a successful interview, be able to assume selected postures or facades without injuring the core of your character (Dexter).

Interviewees frequently say, "I don't want to get involved." While this statement may reflect a desire to protect themselves, occasionally it also means that they want to protect another person. Knowing the inner self of someone else is a sacred trust, and respondents hesitate to reveal information. Therefore, interviewing someone about a third person's actions may be extremely difficult because of the interviewee's loyalty to the third party. The investigator must help the interviewee overcome his or her reservations, and persuade the interviewee that he or she serves the third party's ultimate benefit despite any immediate damage.

Authority and Power

In its simplest form, power is the ability to control, influence, or cause others to do what you want them to do. Authority is the vested, or conveyed, right to exercise power over others. Investigators wield power and authority granted them by the public or private sectors. Because power and authority hold the potential for great misuse, they carry a heavy responsibility to use them legitimately.

What I call authoritarian interviewers grossly misuse their power and authority. They demand absolute obedience without regard for the individual rights and freedoms of others. When crossed, authoritarians become intolerant. They threaten interviewees, describe the steps they will take if the interviewee does not cooperate, and warn of consequences if the interviewee persists. Arrogantly passing judgment, authoritarians humiliate interviewees and strip them of self-respect. Authoritarians expect to be treated like gods, and often are, because of the power they hold to affect the lives of others. But these egomaniacs lack an awareness of their real selves. I have found that a person who has a poor self-image tends to misuse authority. If you doubt your own worth as an individual, you are more likely to act out in destructive ways, building your power by destroying others. I view such egomaniacs as corrupt, prejudiced, sadistic opportunists exploiting their positions of power to earn the respect of their peers (Adorno).

Authoritarians get frustrated a lot because their techniques don't work. To argue with interviewees is self-defeating. For interviewees, information is power. Faced with a threatening authoritarian, interviewees rarely see any constructive advantage in giving up what little power remains to them. The overbearing, contemptuous tactics of the authoritarian are not recommended in this text.

The interviewing techniques suggested in this book are intended to encourage your use of positive authority in everything you do—from the tone of your voice to the way you actively listen. If you trust yourself and know your value as a human being, you can interact with interviewees in positive and productive ways. It is too easy to use harsh, abrasive methods. Instead, strengthen your willpower so that you can avoid entering into a power struggle with interviewees; a power struggle will only create alienation instead of a productive rapport. A positive authority in interviewing encourages self-esteem and cooperation in the interviewee, and promotes confidence and accomplishment in the interviewer.

My intent is not to strip investigators of legitimate authority. It is to encourage investigators not to desecrate or corrupt the power they hold. A community's power rests in the hands of the police officer who enforces the law. I am suggesting tactics which may assist in the positive implementation of such enforcement. Remember, power and authority carry responsibility.

DECEPTION

Before we explore deception, we should establish some criteria for credibility. The credibility of interviewees is based on their truthfulness and believability, and it is related to their observation skills and accuracy in reporting. In order to form a base for further interrogation, the investigator should clarify the following items in the early stages of the interview:

1. Was the interviewee present and aware during the incident? Presence includes more than being there physically. The interviewee might have been "present" by means of a telephone or binoculars. Awareness relates to age, intelligence, or physical state. An adult may be able to describe the chain of events behind an assault; a child may comprehend only that "Daddy hit Mommy."

2.   Was the interviewee attentive during the incident? Distinguish the interviewee's actual experience from his or her feelings about what was observed.
3.   How well-developed are the interviewee's powers of observation? Can the interviewee relate the facts briefly, correctly, and clearly without showing signs of emotional disturbance?
4.   Does the interviewee's nonverbal behavior signal deception?

Frequently, despite our best efforts to make interviewees comfortable with the interview, for a variety of reasons they may still be unwilling to divulge information. Deception is the intentional act of concealing or distorting the truth with the intent to mislead another person into a false judgment. Interviewees deceive when they willfully decide to hide from the investigator what they saw, or what they did, and why. Be alert to signs of the interviewee's mental processes. As you listen attentively to what interviewees have to say, continually observe the ways they act. Through mannerisms, gestures, recurrent phrases, and modes of expression, interviewees often signal their thinking, their needs to protect themselves, and, therefore, their attempts to deceive. Listen for clues to the interviewee's motivation. Indirect questions often provide ways to explore and reveal the interviewee's thoughts, needs, and values. Nourish interviewees' feelings of security and dignity to encourage them to talk and share their thoughts. In the end, the chore for the investigator is not to know the exact reason why the thief stole. Rather, it is to have the thief confess, citing any reason at all, as long as the confession is voluntary and trustworthy. We are really talking about a complex mix of why they committed the crime and why they try to lie to cover up their involvement. To completely comprehend this mix of reasons is not important. But knowing such a mix exists is useful as you encourage the interviewee to volunteer the truth.

Psychological Motives for Deception

Interviewees never have to lie. They have a choice, albeit not always a happy one. Even if innocent of a specific crime, telling the truth may result in shame or embarrassment. If indeed guilty, the truth brings punishment. For some people, an interview is an exercise in unappealing self-revelation inviting negative judgments from the listener; for others, the interview is an exercise in survival. So they lie. The untruthful subject evaluates the potential hazards of an interview. They ask themselves how much the interview will jeopardize their self-esteem, not to mention their freedom. And they lie. Interviewees do not want to be considered ignorant or unable to make decisions; they don't want to be considered immature or unwise. Trying to preserve a self-image, a reputation and ranking among their peers, they work hard to keep their dignity. They lie. Interviewees react to how they are being treated, and when they feel accepted, they don't lie as much, but tend to tell the truth.

We particularly need this sense of comfort, this feeling of being understood, in order to change, elaborate, or clarify a story. "Once having made a general conclusion, a witness is not likely to report individual facts inconsistent with that conclusion" (Binder and Price, p. 134). In other words, an interviewee may have offered a summary of what she thought happened; after further thought, she remembers a fact previously forgotten, or a piece of information previously omitted. If the interviewer has too eagerly accepted the conclusion, and the subject fears being thought silly, the interviewee will allow the summary to stand as accurate. If the interviewee senses that you will "jump all over him" if he clarifies his story, he probably won't. Never challenge the interviewee's veracity before you have accumulated sufficient data with which to do so. Give interviewees some emotional room to maneuver; they appreciate being allowed to save face and have the opportunity to give a fresh, more accurate story.

Just as the interviewee brings a background of experiences into the interview situation, so too does the investigator. "There is a tendency for all of the persons involved in the case to present their data in a manner that meets their own needs" (Abrams, p. 45). The investigator must, therefore, guard against developing any bias based on the reports of anyone, including attorneys, police, witnesses. "This impartiality is particularly important to prevent making unconscious opinions known" to interviewees and affect them accordingly (Abrams, p. 45).

Defense Mechanisms

Rationalization   To rationalize is to invent plausible explanations for actions. Interviewees protect themselves with rationalizations when they hold hidden images of themselves that the facts of their status do not support (Nierenberg). Be sensitive to the possibility that the very nature of interrogation causes interviewees to realize they have not lived up to their personal expectations (Bennis et al). If they feel that by revealing themselves their cooperation purchases low self-esteem, they will probably not be forthcoming. Few people are self-confident enough to be completely indifferent to insults and criticism. If you accept their rationales, you can help interviewees feel moderately confident and, thereby, be more likely to gain needed information.

Researchers have pointed out that, "Characteristically, people look to themselves as the source of their successes and to the situation as the source for their failures" (Downs et al., p. 224). The situation is often one produced by peer pressure—one of the strongest influences on behavior. An individual maintains his or her self-image by conforming to peer pressure, which can produce feelings of conflict and guilt when group behavior contradicts conscience. The subject may feel that she has lost control of her life by subordinating her qualms of conscience to her desire to belong to a group. Hence, interviewees rationalize their actions, not wanting to expose their dependency on conformity (Berg and Bass). You will gain more cooperation if you help lessen their feelings of self-doubt. Proficient interviewers encourage respondents to look at circumstances optimistically, diminishing the negative event through a look or gesture, and encouraging interviewees to reveal the information you need. You might suggest that the interviewee's action (or lack of action) is not so unique after all, that many people have temporarily lost control (Wicks and Josephs). Although you are diminishing the significance of their acts, you are not overlooking the total effect of the act on society and on their lives. Your response merely allows for the free flow of information.

Projection   The dynamics of projection relate closely to rationalization. People generally shift onto others those responsibilities not adequately handled (Wicks and Josephs). When we cannot live up to expectations, we blame others for our behavior. We project onto the victim, the blame for our crime. The person stole the money because someone tempted her by leaving it out on the table; shame on the tempter. The sexual molester abused the child because the child was seductive; shame on the child. When interviewees project, they try to make their behavior understandable and socially acceptable. Thus, it is always someone else's fault, someone else who deserves blame (as seen in the film, *Empathy in Police Work*). Allow respondents to blame other people or the situation. The responsibility is unchanged, but you are closer to hearing the facts of an event.

Warning Signs of Deception

Attempts to deceive create stress, and interviewees display this stress through their verbal responses, nonverbal behavior, and physiological reactions during the interview. Some people can't stand the tension of trying to deceive and readily admit the truth. While a few interviewees are capable of maintaining astonishingly good control over both their verbal and nonverbal responses, most display telltale signs of deception.

Verbal Signs Truthful interviewees display a consistent recollection of details and attempt to dig up related specifics, often offering more than requested. Instead of trying to protect themselves, they feel intellectually challenged to present facts, and they allow the investigator to see their mental wheels turning. They will clearly explain the sequence of events in their efforts to be accurate. With encouragement, they remember details that they thought they had forgotten. They signal their truthfulness through the thoughtful recounting of facts, flowing narration, and acute memory. Even if they become angry after being inconvenienced or embarrassed by the interview, the interviewer can usually quell their anger by remaining controlled and reasonable. Deceptive interviewees, on the other hand, may feign anger to hide their deception, and will not be calmed down, intending to put you on the defensive.

Only skilled actors can lie in a believable manner—and then only with a very limited summary of the facts. The deceptive offer convoluted answers or sophisticated evasions. They take a protected stance, knowing that the less they say, the less likely it is that they will be caught in a lie. A person who has relevant information in an interview, but is not willing to divulge it, must make a conscious effort to keep the truth submerged. He or she disguises this effort as thoughtful contemplation, after which he or she "can't remember." Truthful interviewees rarely say this. Deceptive individuals answer more evasively than the truthful. They use phrases like, "I would deny that allegation" and "I can't tell you much about that."

The deceptive are openly defensive. Their retorts are impulsive and unthinking. They shield themselves with justifications and rationalizations, blaming others or the circumstances. When interviewees begin with the words, "To be honest . . ." or, "To tell the truth . . ." or, "Frankly . . ." or, "Honestly . . .," they most likely intend being neither frank nor honest. Interviewees who express objections, rather than denials, when questioned also are probably not being completely truthful. Interviewees who were later shown to be lying have said the following:

- "I have plenty of money in the bank. I would have no reason to take that money."
- "I'm not the kind of person who would think of doing that."
- "I don't go around doing those kinds of things."
- "I couldn't do something like that."

The objections tend to be true, at least in part. The interviewee who uttered the first objection may actually have had money in the bank, but his response was not a clear denial of his having stolen money. Honest denials are straightforward and crystal clear: "No, I didn't."

Nonverbal Signs When attempting to deceive, some interviewees answer questions and immediately look searchingly at your eyes and face for any non-verbal signs of your skepticism. This subconscious, questioning, wide-open look lasts only a fraction of a second. As the deceptive try to cover the outward signs of lying, the tone of voice may convey internal struggles by sounding unnatural. When interviewees twist the truth, they leave clues in their facial and body movements. A mere twitch or the effort to control a barely perceptible movement is enough indication to warn that something is inconsistent and possibly a fabrication (Davis).

During the time deceptive interviewees pretend to ponder questions, they may engage in some physical action that signals their desire to escape from the interview—mentally if not physically. This form of tension relief may manifest itself as shuffling their feet, or crossing their legs, or covering their eyes. Deceptive interviewees often avoid eye contact by looking around the room or at the floor, frequently picking real or imagined lint from their clothes. In addition, they blink more often than truthful interviewees. They may appear calm—but in a forced way. Although they smile and look composed, the deceptive often seem physically restrained. Their bodies reflect the rigid emotional shells they construct to control their responses. They do not seem spontaneous and flexible, but rather, overly controlled, repetitive, and stifled, with movements that lack complexity and variety. Interviewees who engage in rehearsed gestures without putting their bodies into motion in a smooth, convincing manner signal that their accompanying verbal remarks are probably false. Inappropriate smiles or compliments signal efforts to appease. Some interviewees will flirt inappropriately with the interviewer, trying to distract and divert him or her from the investigation. The deceptive present a false image for you to believe.

A POLYGRAPH EXAMINATION OF A BUDDY

An investigator brought a suspect to me for a polygraph examination. The case involved the sexual molestation of a child. The suspect was a police officer and the investigator introduced him to me as a fine fellow and a good friend. The investigator walked alongside the suspect with his arm around his shoulders in a reassuring way. Such treatment gave me the impression that the investigator had full confidence in the suspect's innocence and was going through the examination as a mere formality. At the time, I was alarmed by such treatment, and it became clear that it only buttressed the suspect's awareness that he needed to hide the truth rather than disappoint his buddy and lose his friendship. I maintained a neutral role and allowed all of the related emotions and fears—shame, professional dishonor, and so forth—to play on the suspect's mind during the polygraph examination. In my opinion, the polygraph examination indicated deception, and in fact the suspect eventually confessed to me that he had sexually molested his daughter. Remember to remain neutral in your search for the truth.

The truthful, on the other hand, even though they may feel uncomfortable about being included in the investigation, are open and straightforward in their manner and speech. Truthful interviewees easily make eye contact with the interviewer. They use free-flowing arm, hand, and body gestures that vary in intensity. Their behavior does not seem rigid or forced in any way; their eyes move freely, and their speech flows smoothly.

Physiological Signs

It is not unusual for the deceptive to exhibit symptoms of physical shock while answering questions, including light-headedness and numbness in the extremities because of reduced blood circulation (see following box on Autonomic Nervous System). These physiological symptoms may be forms of escaping, evidence of their terror when trapped and don't know what to do. They may also exhibit physiological symptoms such as burping, sweating, crying, and appearing to be in a state of turmoil. Truthful individuals generally do not undergo such stress when questioned, particularly if the interviewer stays calm and restrained. Stanley Abrams best describes the emotional triggers of physiological changes.

> Fear is the major activator of [these] physical change[s]. The penalty for being caught in a criminal activity is reasonably clear. The threat of imprisonment, financial loss, or personal embarrassment are sufficiently obvious [to the interviewee] so that no life-long conditioning process is necessary to explain the fear response. While fear is the emotion most likely to [surface] during deception . . . conflict and guilt can also alter the physical state of the individual. . . . Conflict causes tension or anxiety that, like guilt and fear, activates the body processes. During interviews, culpable people tend to have more tension and related physiological changes such as blushing, sweating palms, and other reflections of internal turmoil. . . . The autonomic nervous system causes certain behavioral changes which may be evident to the observant investigator as possible signals of deception.

Fear and conflict are inherent responses, but what a person reacts to is learned. Guilt, on the other hand, is a learned response that had its beginnings in early childhood. Parents, church, and important people in a child's life teach a specific set of values, attitudes, and morals. These teachings are begun early and taught so thoroughly that they become very firmly ingrained within the person. Every time he goes against their teachings, he punishes himself through guilt until he, like most people, functions within the bounds of his conscience (Abrams, pp. 44-45).

Polygraphs and Interviewing

THE AUTONOMIC NERVOUS SYSTEM

Many of the physical symptoms you see during an interview are involuntary reactions produced by a branch of the body's Autonomic Nervous System, called the Sympathetic Nervous System or the SNS. Stanley Abrams explains the process this way.

[The SNS produces] sympathetic arousal [which] is brought about through a threat situation of any kind. . . . The SNS is associated with . . . what Cannon called the flight or fight reaction and serves to temporarily increase and mobilize an organism's energy supply . . . initiating reactions that are concerned with the protection of the individual. . . . During sympathetic arousal the digestive processes stop, including salivation, which accounts for the dryness of the mouth during fear states. . . . Vasoconstriction takes place in the peripheral blood vessels and causes an increased flow of blood to the skin. . . . The arterioles (smaller arteries) are constricted, which . . . raises the blood pressure. . . . In the lungs the bronchia dilate to allow for a greater intake of oxygen. There is an

(continued)

increase in both the heart rate and the strength of the contractions. . . . The pupils of the eyes dilate and the eyes accommodate for distant vision. Perspiration in the 'emotional sweating areas'—the palms of the hands and soles of the feet—increases probably to allow for more effective locomotion and grasping. . . . Fear and anger stimulate the body to perform at levels that are not ordinarily available, and we often hear of remarkable acts of endurance and strength that could not generally be achieved. Sympathetic arousal clearly serves to assist the person in coping with stress. It is an immediate reaction to a threat of any kind. . . . Stress associated with the fear of lying being detected activates a portion of the nervous system, [which, in turn, causes a series of physiologic changes to take place]. . . . From variations in responses related to truthfulness and lying, the polygraphist can deduce with a high degree of accuracy the veracity of each examinee. Lying is not measured by the polygraph per se, but changes in the examinee's body reactions related to the stress associated with deception. . . . In a polygraph examination, the examinee's generalized anxiety raises his level of sympathetic activity, but when his emotional state is aroused during the telling of a lie, a much greater physiologic response will be generated. . . . The affective state involved can be fear, shock, anger, guilt, conflict, or generalized excitement (Abrams, pp. 45-50).

Deception and Psychological Disorders   Pathological liars are people who habitually tell lies so exaggerated, so bizarre, that they are suggestive of mental disorder. They fabricate when it would be simpler and more convenient to tell the truth. Their stories are often complex rationalizations of self-vindication. They are recognized because of their continued fabricated lies throughout life (Cameron and Cameron). The pathological liar weaves lies throughout the fabric of daily life as he or she goes about satisfying human needs, even those as basic as food and shelter.

The psychopathic personality develops along asocial and amoral lines and cannot adjust to society's standards. The psychopath is supremely selfish, and lives only for immediate gratification without regard to the consequences. Normal individuals often sacrifice for the possibilities of the future, and show a willingness to defer certain gratifications. Psychopaths have no understanding of, and even express contempt for, the future. Dr. E. W. Cocke says about the psychopath: "He is always able to differentiate between right and wrong and usually is well acquainted with the requirements of society and religion, but he is absolutely unwilling to be governed by these laws. . . . The only interest which he has with laws is to see that he is not caught in their violation, and, if he is caught, to try to secure, by some trick, a minimum punishment. . . . the only individual that he completely loves, is himself, and he is surprisingly hardened to the rest of the world, including . . . his own family" (Cocke, p. 13).

Researcher George N. Thompson has pointed out, "The secondary [characteristics,] . . . the lack . . . of discretion, judgment and wisdom, impulsiveness, peculiar ability to ingratiate himself, and inability to profit by experience (Thompson, p. 42). Neither long terms in prison nor restraint in psychiatric hospitals affect their conduct.

There is no satisfactory treatment for psychopathic personality. Psychiatrists have, so far, been unable to do any good once the behavior pattern has been established, and researchers have little hope. Appearing self-assured, the psychopath is often a cunning and convincing liar. His or her responses are not too strong, too defensive, or out of context; the motivation is to outsmart the investigator. Still, they can be caught, because as Stanley Abrams says, "the fear of detection [still] exists and probably accounts for their reactivity" during polygraph tests (Abrams, p. 44).

REVIEW QUESTIONS

Answer each of the following questions, and explain your answer fully.

Evidence and the Affective Interview

1. What is the most useful evidence, generally?

2. What is affective interviewing?

3. Are all humans equipped with the same basic needs and defenses?

Universal Human Needs

1. What are Maslow's categories of the human needs underlying behavior?

2. What must we do to be truly adult and efficient?

Safety and Security

1. Where does the child learn values, attitudes, and morals?

2. What are some social norms most people are taught?

3. Why is it beneficial to avoid being judgmental during an interview?

4. When might anger take place in the interview, and what are its effects?

Loving and Belonging

1. What part does conversation play in the satisfaction of human needs?

2. Name three interpersonal needs.

Self-Actualization and Esteem

1. What is the self?

2. What is esteem?

3. What is self-esteem?

4. Why will it be helpful for you to recognize the dignity and worth of the interviewee?

Deception

1. How do you begin to establish an interviewee's credibility?

2. What is deception?

Psychological Motives for Deception

1. Why do people lie?

2. How is saving face important to people?

Defense Mechanisms

1. What does it mean to rationalize?

2. What does projection mean?

3. Is it important to empathize with the interviewee's attitudes and role-playing?

Warning Signs of Deception

1. How do the deceptive typically answer questions?

2. How do the truthful typically answer questions?

3. What is the significance of an subject responding with objections rather than denials?

4. What type of eye contact is typical of the truthful?

Physiological Signs of Deception

1. How does the subject's autonomic nervous system assist your interrogation?

2. What is the flight or fight reaction in the interview environment?

3. How does sympathetic arousal assist a person to cope with stress?

4. What is measured by the polygraph?

5. What is the difference between the psychopath and the pathological liar?

6. What are three of the many symptoms which characterize psychopaths?

REFERENCES

Abrams, Stanley. *A Polygraph Handbook For Attorneys*. Lexington, MA: Lexington Books, 1977.

Bennis, W.G., D.E. Berlew, E.H. Schein, and F.I. Steel, eds. *Interpersonal Dynamics: Essays and Readings on Human Interaction*. 3rd Ed. Homewood, IL: Dorsey Press, 1973.

Berg, Irwin A., and Bernard M. Bass, eds. *Conformity and Deviation*. New York: Harper and Brothers, 1961.

Binder, D.A., and S.C. Price. *Legal Interviewing and Counseling*. St. Paul: West, 1977.

Cameron, Norman, and Ann Margaret Cameron. *Behavior Pathology*. Boston: Riverside Press, 1951.

Cocke, E. W., Dr. "Constitutional Psychopathic Personality in Relation to Present-Day Crime and Delinquency" *The Peace Officer*, Vol. X, No. 1, p. 13.

Davis, Flora. *Inside Intuition*. New York: New American Library, Times Mirror, 1975.

Dexter, Lewis Anthony. *Elite and Specialized Interviewing*. Evanston, IL: Northwestern University Press, 1970.

Downs, Cal W., G. Paul Smeyak, and Ernest Martin. *Professional Interviewing*. New York: Harper and Row, 1980.

Empathy in Police Work. Film. Madison, CT: L. Craig, Jr., producer, 1972.

Maslow, Abraham H. *Motivation and Personality*. New York: Harper, 1954.

Menninger, William C. *What Makes an Effective Man.* Personnel Series no. 152. New York: American Management Association, 1953.

Nierenberg, Gerard I. *The Art of Negotiating.* New York: Cornerstone, 1968.

Thompson, George N. *The Psychopathic Delinquent and Criminal.* Springfield, IL: Charles C Thomas, 1953.

Wicks, Robert J., and Ernest H. Josephs, Jr. *Techniques in Interviewing for Law Enforcement and Corrections Personnel.* Springfield, IL: Charles C. Thomas, 1972.

2

Preparing for the Interview

THE IMPORTANCE OF A POSITIVE ATTITUDE

The more effective you are in collecting testimonial evidence in an interview, the more proficient you will be as an investigator. The attitude you bring to each interview is critical—a positive attitude plays a more essential role than any procedure or technique.

Attitudes form the basis for how we look at ourselves and others. Just as the color and aroma of food influence our enjoyment of a meal, attitudes flavor our efforts to satisfy our needs, and influence our enthusiasm and proficiency. We learn our attitudes in childhood and reinforce them throughout life by our experiences with other people.

Attitudes predispose us to behave in certain ways. Participants on both sides of the interview hold attitudes of trust or skepticism, prejudice or tolerance toward each other, and these attitudes affect how we respond to each other. Your attitude toward the interviewee determines how you treat him or her, and how you treat the interviewee, to a large extent, determines how he or she responds. Clearly, the response you want is full and open cooperation. The most likely vehicle for reaching this goal is a positive attitude.

Elements of a Positive Attitude

The personal characteristics of "warmth, empathy, acceptance, caring, liking, interest, [and] respect [toward] others" (Cameron and Cameron, p. 233), plus the ability to project these qualities will help you become a successful interviewer. Although your primary goal is to obtain truthful evidence, your secondary goal is to make the interviewee feel comfortable, especially to calm their fears. This is true even in investigative interviewing. Most interviewees have no responsibility for the crime. They need you and the information you gain in your interviews to prove them innocent. You can successfully interview by incorporating three main qualities in your positive attitude: empathy, unconditional positive regard, and congruence. We will discuss these qualities first, and then turn to the ways they work in interviewing. If you do not possess these characteristics, try to acquire them:

- Congruence. To be in congruence with yourself means to have a feeling of wholeness about yourself, a feeling that all of your emotional, intellectual, and physical parts fit together in a satisfactory way. Be aware of your feelings and confident enough to express your humanity so that you can communicate with interviewees in a constructive way. To be in congruence with the interviewee means to recognize and accept the human similarities we all share, the needs we try to fill, and the goals we set for ourselves. As we saw in the previous chapter, despite markedly different behavior, we all have the same hopes and fears. Use this sense of congruence to establish empathy.

- Empathy. This quality describes an ability to identify with someone else, to vicariously experience what he or she has experienced. Successful interviewers understand an interviewee's feelings and attitudes toward an event as if they had gone through it themselves. Furthermore, by commiserating with the interviewee, they convey their empathy (Woody and Woody).

- Unconditional positive regard. This attitude reflects the respect due all human beings just by virtue of their being alive. Similar to the unconditional love that parents feel for their children, it is a respect with no strings attached. Regardless of the inquiry, and even when dealing with unsavory interviewees, treat every interviewee as a valuable human being. Develop a genuine liking for people and be tolerant of human weakness. There is no reason why you should feel embarrassed, as if you were violating your personal code of conduct, by adopting an attitude of unconditional acceptance toward others. Most skillful investigators, while they neither condone criminal acts nor excuse criminals, still know the necessity of projecting a positive regard.

The Positive Attitude's Effect on the Behavior of Others

The interviewer's attitude directly affects the outcome of the interview. An interviewee's willingness to cooperate stems more from the interviewer's attitude than from any other factor. All interviewees evaluate the investigator's style, attitude, and expectations. If your attitude is positive, it is far more likely that the subject will respond positively. When you are receptive and un derstanding, responsive and involved, interviewees will more probably enter into a dialogue with you. Let's look at how you can use positive attitudes to create successful interviews.

MAKING THE POSITIVE ATTITUDE WORK

THE CASE OF NIGHT CLERK THEFT

Investigators often allow themselves to be misled by biases fed by appearances. In this case, someone had stolen money from a cabinet in a motel. The police investigator brought three suspects to see me for polygraph examinations. The investigator was focusing on one man who had a history of bringing women into the motel at night for sexual encounters in vacant rooms, and was known to have smoked pot. The investigator made it clear that he did not expect the main suspect to pass the polygraph. When I reported that the main suspect's examination indicated no deception, the investigator reluctantly accepted the report with a shrug, but I sensed that he didn't really believe my evaluation. He said the first man remained his focus although he would bring in two other remote suspects. The polygraph examination showed deception on the part of an eighteen-year-old motel employee who was an excellent student and an outstanding employee. This young man was headed for college the next fall and, until the examination, had not been a real suspect in the eyes of the investigator.

Early on in this case, the investigator made up his mind that the womanizing, pot-smoking night clerk was guilty of the theft. Fortunately, I had more than my opinion to offer: I had a signed confession from the eighteen-year-old that confirmed the innocence of the other two suspects.

Tolerance Versus Prejudice

Unconditional positive regard feeds tolerance, an attitude free of negative judgments. Prejudice toward certain groups of people combined with intolerance of their behavior, hinders the interviewer's effectiveness, as in "The Case of Night Clerk Theft" in the previous box.) "Biases and prejudices can distort perceptual judgments without any conscious awareness or intent to distort information" (Binder and Price, p. 50). The interviewer projects his or her prejudice verbally as well as nonverbally through gestures, changes in posture, tone of voice, and intensity of expression.

People have an amazing ability to sense if you are prejudiced against them (see the Intuition section later in this chapter). Even truthful interviewees who anticipate a negative experience with an investigator will be anxious about your ability to be fair, and, therefore, unresponsive. But interviewees become responsive in a permissive atmosphere. Remember, interviewees are not all good or all bad; therefore, profit by resisting prejudice and open condemnation. Particularly when you feel most critical of an interviewee's behavior, try and superimpose a veneer of tolerance; allow the interviewee to believe that you can accept his or her behavior. The less tolerance you show interviewees, the more they will feel threatened and closed to your questions.

Control your positive and negative bias about those with whom you come in contact. For instance, you know from experience that interviewees frequently lie. But if you convert your knowledge into a bias and treat every interviewee as though you expect a lie, you most likely will shut down any dialogue leading to information. Why should an interviewee tell you anything if you won't believe them? Hold onto your unconditional positive regard of other human beings. By treating each person in a tolerant manner you signal your positive attitude.

Especially when the interviewee exhibits anger or anxiety, the interviewer should display a calm, nonjudgmental attitude. He or she should encourage the interviewee to believe that no attitude is too aggressive and no feeling too shameful to express in the interview. If you can internally forgive the interviewee and show tolerance, you will probably succeed in gaining the necessary testimonial evidence (Wicks and Josephs). You must consider accomplishing your goal as more important than venting your dislike.

Prejudice leads to authoritarianism, an attitude that says you have the right to impose your views on others. It breeds interviewee resentment, retaliation, and a refusal to cooperate. "Some interviewers actually help create the dangerous situations they face by provoking a showdown" (Bennis et al., p. 252). When interviewees feel freedom from prejudice or coercion, their needs to defend themselves are reduced, and you promote productive dialogues.

Curiosity Versus Suspicion

Perceptive interviewees will sense your attitude through the ways you formulate and present your questions. Be a fact gatherer, not a judge. Questions full of genuine curiosity rather than accusatory suspicion further your investigation. Many people find it flattering to be asked for their opinion and will respond with valuable information. Curiosity strengthens rapport and exhibits your respect.

Attitudes are frozen, "and it is with great effort that an unfreezing process" takes place to change those attitudes (Bennis et al., p. 290). If reluctant interviewees exhibit a resentful attitude, ask questions bearing on their hidden resentment rather than the target issue of your inquiry. An indirect route toward your goal may well melt a frozen stance. Try again and again to focus on discovering the truth with different kinds of questions.

Often, especially for young officers, this emphasis on curiosity means that they must learn to focus their energies on the process, rather than the outcome. Remember, if through genuine curiosity, the interviewer learns more about the interviewee than the event, but in the process uncovers the facts of the event as well, the resolution of the investigation automatically follows. Faced with open curiosity, often all an initially uncooperative interviewee needs is patience and encouragement in order to provide truthful information.

Remember that interviewees know that suspicion goes with your job. Investigative interviews necessarily take place to find the truth, and you suspect that each interviewee has some or all of it. Hide your suspicion under curiosity. Undoubtedly, some of the assumptions you make, some of the phrases you use will raise interviewee apathy or hostility. Curiosity generates less hostility than a rigid suspicion of everyone.

Avoid automatically treating each interviewee as though he or she were guilty. Although to trust completely is naive, and you may in fact consider every interviewee deceptive, don't show it. Keep your questions and manner neutral, and hide the fact that you are watching for signs and patterns of interviewee deception. Once you have gathered enough information, you may begin to focus on a particular suspect. Still, try to hold onto your neutral role. If the interviewee becomes offended, he or she will stop cooperating, possibly before you have all the facts you need.

Hiding suspicion is extremely difficult for many of us because we think that challenging a statement will scare the truth out of interviewees. This mistaken belief is the reason we confront so many reluctant subjects who believe that the interviewer takes pleasure in disproving an interviewee's story (Garrett). There is a time to challenge, but not to frighten. Patience will pay off if you remain neutral. You can always interrogate more directly, but do so only after careful observation, evaluation, and assessment of all aspects of the investigation and interview.

INFORMATION IS POWER

The following case is presented as an example of a superior investigator showing empathy and sensitivity to a victim. I was involved in this matter by sheriff's investigators to conduct a polygraph examination of the accused adult. Information related to the crime was reviewed with me in preparation for the examination. The child in the case represents all victims who need the undivided human warmth of an authority figure. On the surface, the

(continued)

child needs a lesson in grammar, but underneath the child needs sympathy and understanding. I believe the questions chosen in this illustration represent what a skilled professional can do.

The case involves an eight-year-old girl who reported being sexually molested by a thirty-seven-year-old family friend. The child first reported the molestation to her father, then to her mother; the parents sought help. A child's verbal skills and maturity do not lend themselves to legal cross-examination in a court of law, so other reasonable proof of the crime and demonstration of the victim's credibility are needed. With her parents and a female social worker present, a male law enforcement investigator interviewed the child. The following extract is from the tape-recorded interview.

> **Question 75:** "What happened?"
> "It sorta hurted when I did."
> **Q76:** "It did? Did it sting?"
> "No."
> **Q77:** Okay, how did it hurt? Can you describe it?
> "Well, it sorta did sting."
> **Q78:** Okay, did you tell your mom that?
> "I just told her it hurted when I went to the bathroom."
> **Q79:** "Has it ever hurted like that before when you went to the bathroom?"
> "Yeah."
> **Q80:** "Was there a reason why it hurted like that before?"
> "Uh-huh."

The above extract illustrates that even young children are aware of how they are being treated. The youngest and least educated among us can sense sympathy or disapproval. A total of 107 questions and answers were involved in the eleven-minute interview. Although the interviewee did not use proper grammar in response to questions 75 and 78, the interviewer did not correct her. Can't you just picture the child warming up to the investigator as the interview proceeds? To help cement a close relationship, the investigator used the child's terminology in questions 79 and 80. As you read the exchange, didn't you rather like the interviewer? No doubt the child heard how the investigator worded the question and on some level of awareness felt a closeness to him. Certainly, rapport was promoted. We can only imagine how the child might have felt if the investigator had corrected her—probably pretty close to how you feel when you're corrected. Remember that on some level we are all children seeking approval and acceptance despite our human failings.

Empathy Versus Judgment

If an interviewee is predisposed to be cooperative and truthful, you may not need most of the methods and techniques suggested in this book. Your professional, nonjudgmental method and positive attitude send a signal to victims, witnesses, and suspects that it is safe to trust you. An "It's-time-to-talk-now" tactic easily directs your investigation. More often, however, this tactic is not enough. You should go further to set the interviewee at ease. You can demonstrate your understanding of the interviewee's needs by actively listening.

To actively listen you should do two things: 1) mentally relax by drawing on your self-esteem and the confidence you have in your own skills; and 2) express a willingness to commiserate and listen. Patience plays a part because interviewees withdraw from hurried indifference. They are keenly aware from your verbal or nonverbal signs if you are reacting negatively. As interviewees express themselves, pay close attention. You might sense some deep emotional hurt that influenced the interviewee's behavior in some way. By comprehending that hurt and putting it into your own words while talking with the interviewee, you show that you are tuned in to the deepest part of him or her. Doing so expresses closeness, and leads to cooperation. (See case in earlier box.)

The language of emotion is subtle but powerful; it doesn't need words. Facial expressions, gestures, mannerisms, and tones of voice transmit feelings and attitudes. This nonverbal communication is learned throughout life, and it signals subconscious attitudes, intentions, and conflicts. We tend to watch for indications of approval or disapproval in the verbal and nonverbal signals we receive from each other. It is striking to note how sensitively interviewees react to the interviewer's mood, approach, attitude, and expectations. Your pause, tilted head, slowly raised eyes to direct eye contact, and slight frown may announce to the interviewee that you are judging, perhaps negatively, his or her answer. Your repositioned stance to a more combat-ready position signals your readiness to do mental, if not physical, battle with the interviewee. Or, you can signal approval and acceptance by an open expression, easy, nonthreatening hand gestures, and a tilt forward in your seat.

When interviewees argue, they are indicating that at least partially, they are considering cooperating. Even interviewees who show up for scheduled interviews and sit quietly without responding to questions signal potential cooperation by their very presence. In this and other difficult situations, try to discover the interviewee's attitudes, needs, and goals. Empathize with interviewees' attitudes, the roles they are playing, and their expressed and demonstrated needs. By acting as a mirror—rephrasing the interviewee's words and reflecting his or her feelings and attitudes—you can signal that you are listening (Nierenberg). We will return to this topic in greater depth in Chapter 4.

Detachment Versus Disgust

Empathy contributes to your ability to assume a neutral facade during interviewing. Learning to empathize can balance your occasionally inevitable disgust at criminal behavior. Remember, it is particularly self-defeating to express your disgust. By degrading interviewees, their efforts, or even their possessions, you promote antagonism. Even if you believe the interviewee is some type of "low life," develop the ability to express yourself in terms that hide how you really feel. Although it is a strain to interact with certain people, sometimes you can produce cooperation only by detaching internally, and externally remaining neutral.

However badly the interviewee has acted, "restrain yourself from lecturing or becoming indignant during the interview" (Woody and Woody, p. 226). Anger and a desire to retaliate tend to cloud your mind, stifle your skills, and limit your inventiveness. Adversarial methods are self-defeating. It is useful to maintain a calm understanding without being ruffled or shocked; be permissive to promote cooperation (Kahn and Cannell).

Try to encourage cooperation by deliberately establishing neutrality (Dexter). If, for example, an interviewee attacks you verbally, avoid retaliation. If challenged, think clearly. From a neutral stance, be objective and tolerant of a certain amount of verbal abuse from rebellious interviewees. Nothing positive is accomplished by responding to their challenges. The successful interviewer listens to the interviewee's comments—whether facts, feelings, speculation, or interpretation—without becoming annoyed or irritated. Being detached helps you to tune into their attitudes while preventing you from responding negatively. If you are detached emotionally you can continue to think clearly and control the situation. It is not appropriate for the interviewer to register surprise at any statement made by the interviewee (Woody and Woody). Indeed, it is counter-productive. A detached interviewer is able to stand aside mentally, make observations about what is going on from moment to moment, and evaluate the situation.

If you display antagonism, fear may cause interviewees to mimic your behavior and attitude. Interviewees who have poor self-images or feelings of inadequacy and helplessness feel great stress under interrogation, and express annoyance, resentment, anger, or hostility. They may engage in lengthy pauses, sudden silences, or an unexplained inability to discuss pertinent details

(Woody and Woody). Avoid an arrogant attitude of condescension or contempt toward the interviewee. If, when communicating, you display a superior stance, interviewees will probably become defensive. A superior attitude tells interviewees that you are not trying to solve a problem, that you do not desire their help or feedback, and that it is likely you will diminish their status and sense of self-worth (Bennis et al.). Make the interview a meaningful give-and-take that increases your effectiveness.

If antagonism develops during an interview, be sure that you have not caused it (Garrett). Monitor your own behavior. As an alert, imaginative individual, you should be able to control yourself so that you will not give the interviewee any excuse to dislike you and block your search for the truth. Naturally, you can't anticipate how each and every interviewee will respond to you, but at least stay alert to opportunities when you can to display positive behavior—the type that will encourage cooperation.

Flexibility Versus Rigidity

Proficient investigators enter each inquiry alert to indications of who committed the crime. Based upon experience, knowledge of human nature, and armed with keen intuitive ability, they can alter or adapt their procedures to meet the requirements of each interview. Clear thinking is the basis of creativity. Creativity and perception can work hand-in-hand toward finding the truth. I am suggesting that you can approach each and every interview with freshness and clarity, with inventive questions and points of view. I consider investigators to be applied scientists who can use their powers of observation, evaluation, and assessment to establish the truth of an inquiry. Skillful investigators approach each investigation as if entering an unknown environment in which they will coax the truth from the participants and crime scene. This is the art and science of interviewing. Immature investigators who are inflexible, and can neither hypothesize nor experiment, tend to be less successful. They do not solve as many crimes because they cannot adapt their skills to the many various interviewees whom they encounter. Being responsive to a wide range of interviewees allows proficient investigators to function most productively. Use your intuition to seize on-the-spot opportunities and do not be inhibited by rigid stereotypes.

Intuition Versus Fact

Knowledge, imagination, and awareness merge into intuition. The seeds of intuitive judgment are probably within you waiting to be discovered, nurtured, and enhanced. Intuition has many common names—gut feeling, hunch, sixth sense, or quick insight. It is the power of knowing through the senses, without recourse to inference or reasoning. The American anthropologist Edward Sapir wrote: "We respond to gestures with an extreme alertness and, one might say, in accordance with an elaborate code that is written nowhere, known by none, and understood by all" (Sapir, pp. 533–543).

Most people possess a remarkable sensitivity to other people, but their intuition remains dormant because they have never exercised it. Yet, intuition proves a valuable tool in interviewing. The spontaneous investigative pathways triggered by your intuition direct the interview. It is your intuitive judgment that guides how you respond to the immediate situation, a new action, or a striking reaction.

Interviewees too are intuitive, and it would be foolhardy to ignore their ability to sense your judgments. In fact, the heightened need to defend themselves that comes with being a suspect of an investigation is likely to stimulate their intuition. Keenly alert to any signals, they respond positively or negatively to what they sense about you and your expectations. They intuit your every move and gesture, your questions and reactions to their answers. "In the course of this intuitive process, [interviewees] bring into play their own values" (Binder and Price, p. 152) and try to gauge the cost of cooperation to their self-esteem. If their intuition tells them they will suffer loss of esteem by cooperating, they most likely will not.

It is vital to acquire a careful balance of the scientific and intuitive so that you can avoid rigid procedures in your interviews. Use intuition as your primary tool in interviewing, allowing it to guide you through various sensitive matters. Otherwise you will be ineffective and unprepared for the spontaneous developments of most interviews. As the Greek philosopher Heraclitus said around 500 BC, "If you expect not the unexpected, ye shall not find the truth." Since seeking truth is your primary objective, expect the unexpected.

Trust yourself to understand what your intuition senses. Seemingly insignificant messages may help you find the information you need. Bodily tension, flushing, excitability, frustration, evasiveness, and dejection can either confirm or deny the interviewee's words. Actively listen by drawing on the storehouse of experience in your subconscious.

At first you may not comprehend the apparently arbitrary techniques used by skilled interviewers. They frequently cannot explain the role of intuition in their interviewing process. Still, proficient interviewers know to confidently nurture intuitions and act on them. They sense an interviewee's tension and spontaneously decide what words or actions will relax the tension and encourage truthful responses. If you want to follow their example, you will have to work at expanding your intuition. Your hunches cannot bear fruit until you put them into action. Initially, rely on self-confidence, follow your gut feelings, and be prepared to learn from your success or failure. As you work through the various steps of interviewing, use the accepted methods, but work at developing intuitive talents and techniques. A good balance is required. Acquiring a mental storehouse of information about human behavior is a must. With that comes greater success. Ask yourself the following questions:

- Do I plan each interview in advance?
- Do I convey a calm composure?
- Do I realize that accepting other human beings does not mean condoning antisocial behavior?

- Do I exhibit sincere interest in the interviewee, and not the boredom of going through routine motions?
- Do I realize that interviewees in their secret and sometimes bashful ways are searching for a signal from me that it is indeed okay to be open and reveal themselves?
- Do I consciously provide positive signals that the interviewee can count on my fairness and tolerance?
- Do I realize that I may subconsciously project dislike and censure during interviews, and trigger hostile feelings, threaten rapport, and set the stage for the interviewee to terminate the interview?
- Do I maintain a positive neutrality to prevent displaying negative signals to interviewees?

CHANGING YOUR ATTITUDES AND BEHAVIOR

In the 1800s, William James, philosopher and psychologist, said, "The greatest revolution [has been] the discovery that human beings, by changing the inner attitudes of their minds, can change the outer aspects of their lives." As a professional, you can make a decided effort to modify your attitudes and change your behavior. Understanding interviewees' cultural attitudes can help you mold yourself more adequately to their personalities and handle their potential reluctance to cooperate. Direct your full attention to the interviewee, and avoid indifference. Remember that what you say and how you say it reflects the perspective you bring to the interview. Your attitude will directly influence the interviewee's responses.

A significant challenge is to become more aware of your own limitations. The more aware you are of your good and bad characteristics as an investigator the more likely it is that you will make changes to improve yourself. You are in deep trouble as an investigator if you think you know it all. If you are still using the old techniques of badgering people and taking the adversarial stance, then you are behind the times. The interviewee's behavior can be changed only by changing the feelings or thoughts on which the behavior is based. In most instances, interviewers lack the time, training, or opportunity to significantly change the interviewee's attitudes. Authoritarians resort to discipline in order to change the behavior itself. Using coercion or duress can only hurt your efforts and may ultimately lead to a civil law suit against you (Yeschke).

If you belong to an organization that uses rigid methods of interviewing you may feel an obligation to do likewise. Yet interviewing tactics that cause anxiety and distress discourage naive, sensitive, and anxious interviewees, while encouraging sophisticated, cynical interviewees to become even more alienated from and distrustful of authority. Consider that if you use Gestapo tactics characterized by insensitive, unskilled, and hollow methods, you are using rigid procedures. In the long run, these tactics will not advance your professional career. You don't have to like to handle distasteful inquiries. Nonetheless, do a professional job when you are faced with such investigations. Adapt to handle all matters, nice or not.

The degree to which you can make a genuine change in your own attitude depends on your predisposition and desire to change. If your coworkers are working toward a positive change of attitude, join in (Bennis et al.). The support of your associates can help you achieve the changes you desire. Discussions among small groups of peers are highly effective in influencing changes of opinion and attitude. An excellent method for developing practical interviewing skills is to have two or more imaginative interviewers pool their ideas. Group role play can be used to test new ideas. This approach allows the less imaginative and less assertive group members to benefit from those who have greater confidence. Overly aggressive interviewers who think highly of their skills with people may learn, to their dismay, that there are interviewees who are more intelligent and more imaginative than they are.

REVIEW QUESTIONS

Answer the following questions, and explain your answers fully.

The Positive Attitude

1. What are the ingredients of a positive attitude?

2. Name several positive attitudes and how they work.

3. If we want to change the outer aspects of our lives, what should we change internally?

Tolerance Versus Prejudice

1. Is it important for the interviewer to be tolerant? If so, why?

2. Can the interviewer's biases be projected?

3. To promote cooperation, does it help to be permissive?

4. Is patience a part of an accepting attitudes? If so, how?

5. Why might even the truthful interviewee be afraid?

6. How can you signal that you are listening?

Curiosity Versus Suspicion

1. How might you arouse fear and defensiveness rather than cooperation?

2. How can you "unfreeze" an interviewee's attitudes?

3. How can using Gestapo tactics affect the interview?

Flexibility Versus Judgment

1. What is the value of being an observational scientist?

2. How does rigidity limit your capabilities?

Intuition Versus Fact

1. What is intuition?

2. Does there seem to be an elaborate code regarding sensitivity to other people?

3. How do you select investigative pathways?

4. How can you put your intuition to work for you?

REFERENCES

Adorno, T.W., Else Frenkel-Brunswik, Daniel F. Levinson, and R. Nevitt. *The Authoritarian Personality*. New York: Sanford, Harper and Brothers, 1950.

Bennis, W.G., D.E. Berlew, E.H. Schein, and F.I. Steel, eds. *Interpersonal Dynamics: Essays and Readings on Human Interaction, 3rd ed.* Homewood, IL: Dorsey Press, 1973.

Binder, D.A., and S.C. Price. *Legal Interviewing and Counseling*. St. Paul: West, 1977.

Cameron, Norman, and Ann Margaret Cameron. *Behavior Pathology*. Boston: Riverside Press, 1951.

Dexter, Lewis Anthony. *Elite and Specialized Interviewing*. Evanston, IL: Northwestern University Press, 1970.

Garrett, Annette. *Interviewing: Its Principles and Methods*. New York: Family Service Association of America, 1972.

Kahn, Robert L., and Charles F. Cannell. *The Dynamics of Interviewing: Theory, Technique, and Cases*. New York: Wiley, 1957.

Nirenberg, Jesse S. *Getting through to People*. Englewood Cliffs, NJ: Prentice-Hall, 1963.

Sapir, Edward. *Selected Writings of Edward Sapir*. D. G. Mandelbaum, ed., Berkeley and Los Angeles: University of California Press, 1949.

Wicks, Robert J., and Ernest H. Josephs, Jr. *Techniques in Interviewing for Law Enforcement and Corrections Personnel*. Springfield, IL: Charles C. Thomas, 1972.

Woody, Robert H. and Woody, Jane D, eds. *Clinical Assessment in Counseling and Psychotherapy*. New York: Appleton, Century, Crofts, Meredith, 1972.

3

The Self-Fulfilling Prophecy

The self-fulfilling prophecy is based on the notion that expectation produces the reality; that is, we achieve what we expect to achieve. The self-fulfilling prophecy bears on interviewing because the expectations with which we approach interviewing tend to be realized. The way we treat people determines, to a large extent, the responses we receive from them. Our expectations alone influence the interviewee in such a way that he or she tends to live up to our expectations. Our expectations can be positive or negative, but, for two reasons, I recommend choosing to approach interviewees with positive expectations. The positive expectation indicates a belief in yourself and a belief that you will succeed. It indicates your belief that all individuals want to be treated as worthwhile human beings and that you expect them to act as if they are. As you treat them, so do they tend to perform. Because you expect to find the truth in your investigative interviews, treat interviewees as though they want to provide you with true information. In the main they will. Conversely, if your expectations are negative, you can produce negative effects. This self-fulfilling prophecy is commonly referred to as the Pygmalion effect (*Productivity and the Self-fulfilling Prophecy*, film) and relates directly to the Galatea effect. We will discuss each in turn.

The Galatea Effect

The Galatea effect refers to the expectations we place on ourselves. These are the prophecies for our own futures that we work to fulfill. The expectation that we will reach the goals we set for ourselves propels us toward them. With each interview I conduct, I aim to make the next one even better, more productive. With each investigation I try to be better organized, smarter, and more proficient. With each achievement, each incremental step forward, I give myself a "pat on the back for a job well done."

It takes courage to discover what we are capable of doing. No one holds our hands or guides us through each step. We must find our ways alone. If productivity as an interviewer and development of successful interviewing techniques continue to be your long-range goals, it will take extraordinary drive and determination to be successful. By raising our levels of self-expectation, we investigators display a self-confidence and self-assurance which are nearly synonymous with each other and with self-esteem. (Gist; Eden and Kinnar). Unfortunately, the Galatea effect can sometimes be negated by others—their expectations of our abilities. Those who are willing to commit themselves to a highly demanding undertaking must have a belief in their capacity to mobilize the physical, intellectual, and emotional resources they will need to succeed.

The Pygmalion Effect

The Pygmalion effect refers to the expectations we have of others and they have of us. Playwright George Bernard Shaw illustrated the theory of the self-fulfilling prophecy in the play, *Pygmalion*, which was adapted as the musical *My Fair Lady*. In this play, Eliza, "a flower girl" from the slums of London, insists that she cannot become the lady Professor Higgins is training her to be until he *sees* her as a lady, instead of just a flower girl masquerading as a lady. Eliza says, "You see, really and truly, apart from the things anyone can pick up [the dressing, the proper way of speaking, and so on], the difference between a lady and a flower girl is not how she behaves, but how she's treated. I'll always be a flower girl to Professor Higgins, because he always treats me as a flower girl, and always will, but I know I can be a lady to you, because you always treat me as a lady, and always will" (Shaw).

Clearly, how we behave toward an individual influences that person's response. Everything we do and say conveys our expectations. If revealed, every positive or negative attitude or belief can convey elements of our expectations. If those elements, when exposed, reveal the disgust and contempt in which we hold the criminal, we risk closing down the interview. If we have little regard for the bad guy, surely such disregard will show itself at some untimely moment and shout at the one we are gently nudging toward the truth. Far more than verbal prodding, the self-fulfilling prophecy encompasses your total behavior, conscious and subconscious. Let's look more closely at this theoretical concept and how you can make your expectations work for you.

THE FOUR ELEMENTS OF THE SELF-FULFILLING PROPHECY

In his dissertation, educator and psychologist Robert Rosenthal showed through scientific experiments that "the power of expectation alone" significantly influences the behavior of others. Drawing on his experience as a teacher, he showed that:

- If he believed the students in his experiments had greater potential, and
- If this belief raised his expectations of them, and

- If he transmitted his expectations to the students,
- Then, as a result, they became higher achievers.

Through studies and experiments, Rosenthal and his associates developed a theory of communicating expectations and broke it down into four elements: climate, feedback, input, and output (*Productivity and the Self-fulfilling Prophecy*, film). We will define and describe each specific behavior below. Remember, each element is an integral part of the whole.

Element I: Climate

The climate communicates your expectations to interviewees through all your nonverbal messages from your body language to your paralanguage. Body language includes mannerisms, gestures, eye contact, facial expression, and body posture; paralanguage encompasses tone of voice and the use of silence. The climate of an interview is in play from the beginning to the end of the conversation. Before you have a chance to speak, you are under scrutiny for signs of acceptance and trust. Some interviewers are adept at using the climate of an interview to allay an interviewee's fears and encourage cooperation. Others must learn to use climate by watching those with skill, and practicing on everyone with whom they come in contact. In the interview itself, deliberate communication of nonverbal messages requires subtle delivery to avoid the appearance of pretense and to avoid arousing the interviewee's suspicions.

Element 2: Feedback

Feedback refers to "the process of correction through incorporation of information about [the] effects of [one's performance]. When a person perceives the results produced by his own actions, the information so derived will influence subsequent actions. Feedback thus becomes a steering device upon which learning and the correction of errors are based" (Reusch, p. 4). In responding to interviewees' feedback, investigators reveal their expectations though active listening and vocal acknowledgment. It is difficult to anticipate how to react to a particular interviewee's feedback because of the unpredictability of some interviewees. Therefore, remember to stay alert, neutral, flexible, and professional. You can channel feedback by emphasizing your input.

Element 3: Input

Input is the distinct, verbal transmittal of the interviewer's expectations. It is the key ingredient of any interview. Prepare your verbal input so that you can establish a clear picture of what you expect from the interviewee. The goal is to set the stage so that it is virtually impossible for the interviewee to surprise or divert you. Your neutral stance in explaining how an interviewee can assist your inquiry is vital to your success.

Element 4: Output

Output is the distinct response from the interviewee. It may be silence, uncooperative behavior, lies, or verbal information. The interviewer communicates his or her expectations of the interviewee's output and encourages or discourages cooperation. If your expectation is negative, you encourage negative responses. But if you remember the self-fulfilling prophecy (the Pygmalion effect) of interviewing, your positive expectation will be rewarded by cooperation.

If the revelation of the truth is the desired output, it is helpful to develop a positive, humane interaction that encourages respondents to comply. Treating interviewees as though they want to provide the greatest degree of truthful cooperation establishes a high probability that they will do so. That is, during the progress of the interview the investigator can encourage the interviewee by paying attention to each comment and thereby nurturing more comments. By overt approval, the interviewer positively acknowledges any information that is offered. Thus the methodology moves from belief and expectation through action and reaction.

APPLYING THE SELF-FULFILLING PROPHECY

Your belief in yourself and your expectation of success should exist side by side before each interview, regardless of the investigative circumstances. These two, belief and expectation, are not open to debate. They should be embedded in your mind's core, rooted deeply in the energy that strengthens you to be daring enough to try and try again to learn the truth with imagination and enthusiasm.

As an investigator gains real-world experience, his or her ability to create useful degrees of belief and expectation increases as their effectiveness in interviewing is confirmed. The development of these two characteristics and the skill in using them builds gradually over the years. There are two practical steps you can take toward acquiring this skill—one intellectual, the other practical:

- Mental belief. Throughout my professional experience of interacting with interviewees, I have used the self-fulfilling prophecy. Before an interview, I take stock of myself and my overall expectations. During this mental exercise, I remind myself that I am a talented and resourceful individual capable of handling a wide variety of inquiries ranging from murder to counter-espionage. I remind myself that this new investigation is much like the others I have handled. I consider what I expect of myself and how I intend to treat the interviewee. Before even knowing the details of the new inquiry, I establish a personal, private strategy, and determine to do the best professional job I can. This helps me set my course and focus my energy. Believe in yourself and your ability to verbally and nonverbally encourage others to provide truthful information. Believe that interviewees are ready, willing, and able to share truthful information. Maintain a positive expectation of success. By everything you think, do, and say, demonstrate that you anticipate receiving cooperation.

- Applied action. When applying the self-fulfilling prophecy during investigations, it is vital to understand the needs, and meet the expectations of, those you investigate (see Chapter 1). Many interviewees are desperately seeking opportunities to explain why they are not so bad or unacceptable despite their having committed a crime. They, too, are expecting something out of the interview. They need you to make it all go away, to make it okay again, to calm the waves of turmoil in their lives, to make it right. They need to know they are still acceptable as human beings and not pieces of trash. They expect you to bring them back into human warmth. Therefore, express an "I'm okay, You're okay" attitude (Harris). When the guilty sense that you may be the one who will allow him or her back into the fold, you may get the truth, or some modification cushioned in rationalization and face-saving.

Remember, interviewees tend to live up to your expectation. Treat interviewees as valuable human beings, regardless of the inquiry, and they will act like valuable human beings. Treat interviewees as though they are more compliant than they appear to be at first glance, and they will be. If your tactics are positive, interviewees will probably comply with your requests for information.

How can investigators demonstrate an "I'm Okay, You're Okay" attitude when dealing with a particularly heinous crime like child molestation? It's certainly not easy. My answer is to pretend that you are playing a role in the theater. Make your performance believable! Avoid being noticeably judgmental. Find some value in the interviewee. Don't allow yourself to outwardly condemn the person. As repulsive as this may seem, help the suspect rationalize his or her involvement in the crime. In a child molestation case, for example, the abuser may want to believe that the child seduced him or her. Go along; disguise your contempt. If he or she senses that you are not neutral, you may not obtain an admission of guilt. This restraint is hard to maintain, no doubt, but it is necessary if you are to be of the greatest service to your community.

Presenting Expectations Subtly

Present your positive expectations of the interviewee's cooperation subtly. Don't actually say, "I know you want to tell me . . . " Simply treat interviewees as though they want to comply. In actuality, interviewees often do not want to cooperate with the investigation—at least not at first and not to the extent that you expect. By acting on a false assumption however—that the interviewee will want to help with your investigation—you turn your expectation into reality. You can persuade them to accept the idea of compliance even though they had determined not to. Sell them on the idea in subtle, thought-provoking ways. You will become more confident as you acquire positive experiences. Success breeds success and your capability to investigate a broad variety of crimes is strengthened by each new accomplishment.

The Galatea Application

The Galatea effect is a boost in personal performance which is based upon self-efficacy—the investigator's judgment of his or her capabilities. This self-efficacy is based on belief, motivation, and performance, and in turn, influences the performance standard you select for yourself. Self-efficacy is not so much to do with the skills you have but your judgment of what you can do with your skills. Self-efficacy arises primarily from the effects of mastery, modeling, and persuasion. That is, self-efficacy is influenced by personal accomplishment, watching others succeed, and being persuaded by yourself and others that you can perform to high standards.

While self-confidence in one's skills is built primarily upon having successfully used these skills in the past, you can also build your skills by watching the behavior of others who are successful and listening to their advice. At first, self-efficacy is task-specific and emanates from the individual's belief that he or she can perform a particular task at a specific level of competence. An important variable in predicting success is an individual's confidence that he or she can master new investigative situations (Gist; Eden and Kinnar). As your experience builds, self-efficacy emanates from your success marked by self-administered rewards. Rewards reinforce accomplishment. If you expect to successfully conclude an investigation, and you then do, it's a good idea to reward yourself in some way. Some reward such as buying yourself an ice cream cone will be a symbolic pat on the back for a job well done. Once established, self-efficacy applies to all investigative situations. Set your goals, observe others, expect positive outcomes, and self-monitor your performance (Gist; Eden and Kinnar).

The Pygmalion Application

One of the important forces in social interaction is the tendency for one person to communicate, verbally and/or nonverbally, his expectations to another person. The second person then tends to respond consciously or unconsciously to those expectations. Certainly this desire to live up to expectations is what lies behind peer pressure. Scientific research in business has verified that people tend to live up to the expectations of others. Industrial psychologists have long realized the necessity of creating management patterns to foster motivation, improve communication, and increase productivity. Case studies show that high expectations lead to high performance and that low expectations result in poor performance. The announcement of the "successful" venture may be a self-fulfilling prophecy (Boorstin).

This evidence illustrates the benefits of applying the self-fulfilling prophecy. According to educator and sociologist Dr. Robert Merton, the self-fulfilling prophecy shows nothing so shallow as the power of positive thinking or magic, but rather the definite social and psychological processes that have a profound effect on interpersonal communication. In investigations we seek a revelation of the truth through conversation. For example, I desire to learn the truth of what happened during a crime. I believe that when I behave in a positive way I encourage the interviewee to respond positively. As a result of my behavior toward the interviewee I will probably learn the truth. The belief and expectation are turned into reality through my efforts. Because of your role in society, your expectations and how you express them can influence the behavior of interviewees. Your high expectation of success with others can produce beneficial results.

REVIEW QUESTIONS

Answer the following questions and explain your answers fully.

The Self-Fulfilling Prophecy

1. Does recognizing another as a worthwhile person have anything to do with the self-fulfilling prophecy?

2. Is the self-fulfilling prophecy also known as the Pygmalion effect?

3. Does your attitude toward interviewees determine how you treat them?

4. Is there a tendency for people to conform to other people's expectations?

5. How do you convey your expectations?

6. What are self-expectations?

7. How can you gain greater proficiency as an investigator?

The Four Elements of the Self-Fulfilling Prophecy

1. How does the climate of an interview communicate your expectation?

2. Does your response to interviewee feedback reveal your expectation?

3. How does your input reveal your expectation?

4. Is the interviewee's output influenced by your input of expectations?

Applying the Self-Fulfilling Prophecy

1. How do you prepare yourself for an effective interview?

2. Can experience help you create useful degrees of belief and expectation?

3. Is your confidence influenced by experience?

4. How can you demonstrate that you expect cooperation?

5. Why is it important to appear neutral during interviews?

6. Is treating interviewees as though they want to comply a way of showing your expectation?

7. Is it important for the interviewee to feel acceptable?

8. How can your behavior encourage interviewee cooperation?

9. What is the relationship of belief to self-efficacy?

10. What influences the development of self-efficacy?

11. What is the impact of how you treat the interviewee in relationship to cooperation?

NOTE

The following authors have explored the benefits of applying the self-fulfilling prophecy: Rensis Likert, social scientist and educator; J. Sterling Livingston, management consultant and educator; Douglas Murray McGregor, social scientist and president of Antioch College; Robert K. Merton, educator and sociologist; Robert Rosenthal, educator and psychologist.

REFERENCES

Boorstin, Daniel. *The Image*. New York: Athenaeum, 1972.

Eden, D., and J. Kinnar. "Modeling Galatea: Boosting Self-Efficacy to Increase Volunteering." *Journal of Applied Psychology* 76/6 (1991): 770–80.

Gist, M.E. "Self-efficacy: Implications for Organizational Behavior and Human Resource Management." *Academy of Management Review* 12/3 (1987): 472–85.

Harris, Thomas A. Videotape. *I'm Okay—You're Okay: A Practical Guide to Transactional Analysis*. Distributed by Success Motivation Institute, New York, by special arrangement with R.M. Karen and Harper and Row, 1973.

Productivity and the Self-fulfilling Prophecy: The Pygmalion Effect. Film. New York: McGraw-Hill Films, 1975.

Reusch, Jurgen, and Weldon Kees. *Nonverbal Communication*. Berkeley: University of California Press, 1954.

Shaw, George Bernard. *Pygmalion*. Dover Publications, Mineola, New York, 1994.

4

Tactical Concepts

Clearly, interviews are not normal social encounters in which two people exchange ideas and experiences on an equal footing. In interviews, the interviewee should do most of the talking while the investigator acts as a catalyst to stimulate recollections and promote their revelation. As the catalyst asks appropriate questions, he or she probes for facts, anecdotes, and impressions from interviewees (Sherwood). The catalyst generates an unspoken chemistry that produces cooperation. To prepare for your role as interviewer-catalyst, look at each inquiry with a fresh eye, and plan your approach. Detach yourself from the emotional content of the interview, adopt a positive attitude, and prepare to be flexible. In your role as catalyst two major techniques will prove useful: 1) to actively listen and, 2) to build rapport. We will look at each technique in turn.

ACTIVE LISTENING

His thoughts were slow, his words were few, and never
made to glisten. But he was a joy wherever he went. You
should have heard him listen.

Anonymous

Mutual confidence and trust are difficult to achieve in interviews, and interviewees are not always your partners. While
your goal is to establish the truth, their goals may be to protect
themselves. A good interviewer is a good listener. The most successful investigators have a self-possession that allows them to
actively listen. Through the use of questioning, accepting,
rephrasing, and pausing, they show that they are listening. They
are alert and courteous, and give the interviewee their undivided
attention. It seems most people are seldom listened to during
their lives, and they appreciate the opportunity to express themselves (Bennis et al.). They hunger for that feeling of importance
when approached for their views.

In addition, interviewees often want to understand the significance of what they have to say to your inquiry. Make your
inquiry a balance between revealing how it relates to an interviewee's life and concerns (Bennis et al.), and discretion about your
overall objective or hypothesis (Dexter). Too much explanation
may subtly direct the interviewees to respond in particular, often
inaccurate, ways, or cause them to worry about the harm their information may cause others.

Avoid putting on a show of authority, taking more interest
in yourself than in your role of listener. Be less demanding and
more understanding. Don't start a battle with the respondent,
but be ready with appropriate questions or comments to show
your interest in what the interviewee has said. My experience indicates that the sifting and extracting of valuable information
takes place by using active listening. This important tactic of active listening requires acceptance of others, detachment, patience, and concentration.

Acceptance of the Interviewee

When you actively listen to interviewees you signal your acceptance of them, and they intuitively sense that you are okay to talk to. Like most people, interviewees often think that what they have to say is the most important thing in the world, and they continually evaluate their listeners. "Probably one of the most powerful actions for implying acceptance of someone is to listen. . . . Good listening takes practice; it's actually a discipline. . . . Listening doesn't come naturally; it has to be developed" (Mallory, pp. 146–51). While interviewees expect and appreciate appropriate responses to their comments, they don't necessarily seek an evaluation. They need reassurance, support, and acceptance while revealing their thoughts and exposing their secrets. Use sounds and actions to signal your acceptance of the interviewee. Murmur vocal sounds such as uh-huh at appropriate times during the interview. Encourage the interviewee's continued recitation by nodding your head to show that you are following them. If the interviewee talks spontaneously, avoid interrupting until there is a significant pause. Remember that participants on both sides of the interview engage in the listening process (Drake), and by expression, tone of voice, or verbal content the sender can seem to be evaluate or judge the listener (Bennis et al). If the listener's response is a blank, far-away look, it can indicate a lack of attention and disassociation from the interview.

The ideal interviewer listens with nonjudgmental understanding and does not criticize or admonish (Garrett). By exhibiting genuine interest, interviewers may avoid injecting their opinions, value judgments, and criticisms into the interview. Remember, when you interview, tuck your personal values away. When interviewees sense that they are being evaluated by you, they become defensive and curtail the flow of information. Let us assume that you passionately believe that anyone who is involved in sexual child abuse, or bank robbery, or drunk driving should be hung by their toes out of a ten story building until they starve to death, or until their toes rot off and they plummet to the cement pavement below. If you express your feelings in the interview, you will not only not get the testimonial evidence you need to take to court, but you will not get justice.

Concentration

One difference between mediocre and first-class interviewers is the ability to combine active listening and analysis with questions that trigger truthful responses. By concentrating, you can acquire this ability. "Hear" interviewees with your total, undivided attention. This is essential in assessing others. There is a close connection between active listening and intuition—to sense meanings that do not come through words. By concentrating, you can determine the interviewee's frame of reference, reduce emotional tension, and generate cooperation.

Avoid idle thinking by concentrating on the specifics of the interview. Get into the mood of data gathering and listen constructively. Allowing the interviewee's comments to glide over the surface of your mind is self-defeating. Concentrate! Preoccupied glances, slack body posture, and the lack of responsive comments all imply boredom. Don't let your boredom show. When facing an inattentive listener, interviewees tend to regard the interview as a waste of time and hold back information. Since they may never outwardly express their reasons for withdrawing, you may never realize that your lack of concentration stopped the flow of information.

Inattentive listeners may not even hear what is being said; they superficially signal hearing, but formulate no real thoughts in response. Sharp, alert, quick replies are missing. The interviewer seems out of step with the discussion, never pausing to reflect on what the interviewee has said, and never quite catching up. Instead of focusing on the moment, the interviewer is thinking up the next question. Concentrate!

As an active listener, your attention should not be fickle, falling apart at the least distraction or promise of pleasure, excitement, or frustration (Nirenberg). In fast-moving interviews, inattentive listeners seem preoccupied. If you don't concentrate your thinking, skilled deceptive interviewees may too easily mislead you. Even illusive interviewees, who are not really deceptive but are only reluctant or hesitant to comply, can mislead you if you don't pay attention. Listening means concentrating on what is and is not being said—both verbally and nonverbally.

Detachment

Occasionally you will need to investigate crimes that are so horrible and disgusting that they shake you to your very core, turn your stomach, and literally make you sick. No matter what the circumstances, however, don't be thrown off balance. Don't become so angry that you want to seek revenge on behalf of the victim. Remain detached; therein lies your real revenge. If you can detach you will treat even the despicable, contemptible dregs of the earth with a productive neutrality. Acknowledge their humanness, and proceed to get the information you need to bring them to justice. Calmly, coolly, pursue the testimonial evidence you need. Avoid any overt threats that may block interviewee compliance. The unschooled investigator tends to use crude behavior they think will work, but which will only frighten one interviewee and amuse the cynical. Eventually these investigators learn that their threats produce defensive reactions that shut down dialogue.

There are times when an interview crumbles, and the tense, anxious investigator, feeling personally incompetent, turns his or her distress against the interviewee by scolding, hitting, or berating the interviewee. Such judgmental behavior may temporarily relieve some of your tensions, but will undoubtedly destroy the prospects of gaining sought-after evidence. By concentrating on the process of gathering the truth, you will avoid self-doubt and build your competence.

Underneath a skillful style you may feel distracted by an intensity of internal dissonance, an absence of internal harmony. When you are expected to remain calm and listen, your body cannot vent the pent-up pressure caused by stress. It is therefore necessary to be alert to the accumulated pressures from your job, romance, or family circumstances. Some investigators break under the stress and injure an interviewee. Don't let this happen to you. The solution? Detach. Be cool! Separate the elements of your life—your professional life from your personal life, the pressures of bureaucracy from the goal of a particular interview—and don't allow access to your "emotional buttons." Make up your mind that no matter what, regardless of the stress, you will be in control of yourself. Use the power of your will to maintain the highest level of professionalism.

Condition yourself to be strong enough emotionally to hear anything the interviewee may want to say. An open listening technique allows all manner of content to enter the discussion. The interviewee may release a blast of emotion while you try to gradually obtain a clear expression of the facts of an event (see Chapter 11 interview with Suanne). Whatever sadness, gloom, or disappointment may be conveyed by the interviewee, detach and listen with your whole being. Through the tears, you may hear some gem of evidence, a fact you can use to solve the investigation.

When interviewees respond in an angry outburst, detach and be ready to withstand the heat. Do not react in a defensive manner. Too often, the interviewer's need to talk is greater than his or her ability to listen. Effective interviewing demands that you overcome this human failing (Benjamin). It is the listening and not the talking that produces the better results. You might say, "I see your point of view," or "I understand what you mean." You will only alienate the interviewee if you react to emotional tirades with threats or insults or fall back on your position of authority and demand that the interviewee remain civil.

Patience

Inexperienced interviewers often rush from one question to the next without waiting for an answer. They fail to understand that patience is a necessary component of active listening. Their rawness gives them tunnel vision as they race to some prescribed goal only to find that they have sped by important information in the process. They need to slow down. Patience is also a necessary component of rapport, and to a large extent, the degree of rapport you establish determines the effectiveness of an interview. Present yourself as the type of person who has extensive experience and deep understanding, the type that is tolerant of human frailties and with enough patience to hear about them. Serenity—a quality of quiet strength to rely on in times of potential tension—is patience at work.

Your patience and indulgence signal tolerance, acceptance, and understanding, while it stimulates dialogue. Built within it, patience carries forgiveness and respect for interviewees. Painstakingly and patiently advance point by point and item by item toward your goal. "Be patient and persistent to overcome hidden, irrational interviewee opposition" (Nirenberg, p. 132). If the interviewee becomes hostile or indignant, try to remain calm and appeal for cooperation. Avoid overt impatience that signals ridicule, cynicism, and intimidation, and blocks rapport. Remember that threats and ultimatums in the service of impatience are self-defeating and abusive. As Benjamin Disraeli, one of Britain's foremost prime ministers, said, "Next to knowing when to seize an advantage, the most important thing in life is to know when to forego an advantage." By being patient you forego an advantage and hold back the wrath you may feel welling up within you.

Your patience is essential in the face of an emotional outburst. A sensitive response to a victim in distress is essential in reducing the victim's fear. Permit interviewees to discharge high-energy, stored emotions of anger and pain in an emotional dumping process. Your patience gives interviewees time to rid themselves of tension as they meander conversationally and test the limits of your patience. The strength you display in a gentle response leads to confidence in your judgment. Be alert to both concrete and abstract information. Concrete, objective explanations paint a clear picture of the event or situation. Abstract, subjective comments are emotional, unspecific, and often misleading. Strive to obtain concrete comments, but accept that the interviewee will also express emotion and make many subjective comments. Take comfort and reassurance from William Keefe's comment that, "Eventually [the investigator] may spend less time as he winnows more skillfully the valuable information from the valueless" (Keefe, p. 24).

As your career progresses, you will come in contact with people who display varying degrees of emotion. Some interviewees are so touchy that they become petulant, irritable, or, at worst, unwilling to talk at all. Some people are so self-centered that they think everyone, including you, should bow to their wishes. Some people know it all and can be most difficult to get along with. Your patience and gentle persuasion can guide the inquiry no matter what personality type you need to interview.

NONVERBAL ACTIVE LISTENING

Active listening involves your whole body. Express your willingness to listen by the tone of your voice, the position of your body, and the expression on your face. Kinesics is the study of the relationship between body motions and communication—in other words, the study of body language. Paralanguage includes vocal effects, such as tone of voice, that carry meaning. Through your body language and paralanguage, you communicate your expectations of and reactions to the interviewee.

Body Language

Body language includes posture, position, gestures, and mannerisms through which we communicate with others. During an interview, your nonverbal behavior is constantly under scrutiny, and a single negative message has the potential to render an interview ineffective. Before you utter your first word, the interviewee will examine you for signs of trustworthiness. Your only defense is to deliver believable signals of acceptance. Nonverbal behavior—including nodding your head, looking curious, moving forward in your chair, and smiling—encourages interviewees to continue speaking. Extreme dislike, a high assertion of dominance, and responsiveness are all expressed through tone of voice, deliberate silences, variations in eye contact, facial expressions, distancing, and posture (Film: *Communication, The Non-Verbal Agenda*).

Body Posture and Movement   Signal that you are paying attention by sharing postures, by standing or sitting close, and by facing the interviewee squarely or at a 45-degree angle. Move slowly and confidently to avoid scaring the interviewee. Leaning forward indicates that you are warm and alert to the interviewee as a human being.

When you sense that you are communicating with an interviewee, moving mentally and physically together, you will have achieved interactional synchrony and will signal attentive listening (Davis). Try to move in time to the rhythm of the speaker. When he shifts, you shift. When he is still, you be still. People are drawn to those who seem to mirror them and share things in common. Just as a perfect meshing of gears is essential to a smooth-running engine, the better the mesh between investigator and interviewee, the more productive the interview. Your part in this flow and rhythm encourages relaxed thinking in the interviewee. Be in synchrony, think on the run without loss of balance, and stay alert to what is happening moment by moment. Vocal intonations, timing, silences, facial expressions, eye movements, and body positioning may confirm, obscure, or contradict spoken words. Such subtle signals, and especially any patterns you note in these signals, may give you good reason to eventually confront the interviewee.

In his article, "Significance of Posture in Communications Systems," Dr. A.E. Scheflen writes, "A position is a gross postural shift involving at least half the body. When the listener reaches a point when he disagrees with the speaker, he shifts his position in preparation for delivering his protest" (Scheflen, pp. 316–331).

When you disagree internally with an interviewee be careful not to announce your disagreement or desire to contradict the interviewee.

Gestures   If your body language is in any way accusatory, for example, by pointing your finger, the interviewee will become defensive. Proficient interviewers use their body language to relay nonconfrontational interviewing tactics. They keep their arms open and their palms extended. At times it is helpful to place your hand on the interviewee's hand, arm, or shoulder in a reassuring way—it can strengthen the bonds of rapport. Proficient interviewers learn to use reassuring touch to exhibit their acceptance of the interviewee and strengthen interpersonal communication. A complicated combination of things occurs, however, when two human beings touch, so be careful to determine when a touch is appropriate. Women, in particular, protect their personal space. Hostile or extremely reluctant interviewees will usually not allow themselves to be touched, if even to shake hands. Some people do not want others to come close to them, and they certainly do not want to be touched. This restraint usually has nothing to do with you personally and probably has nothing to do with the matter under investigation.

Facial Expression and Tone of Voice   Look at the interviewee often and wear an interested or pleased expression. Those muscles that control frowning, pouting, pursing, squinting, and others all combine from time to time to convey your feeling of judgment regarding interviewee information or behavior. You indicate an authoritarian attitude by changes in your speech intonation and tempo; it may be rapid, or you may suddenly turn silent (Woody and Woody). Since facial expressions and tones of voice symbolize subconscious attitudes they influence others' behavior just as powerfully as the words you speak. Phrases like "I see," "Please go on," "Yes," and "Uh-huh" indicate interest and desire to hear more. But the impact of these expressions can be negative or positive depending on how they are expressed. You might say, "Please go on," but stop the flow of information with a tone that proclaims disbelief or boredom. Collect evidence in a fair and impartial manner by keeping your tone alert and neutral.

Positive Silence

"He that has eyes to see and ears to hear may convince himself that no mortal can keep a secret. If his lips are silent, he chatters with his fingertips; betrayal oozes out of him at every pore" (Davis, p. 54). When used appropriately, without an intentional threat to the interviewee, silence can strengthen rapport and encourage compliance. Silence can indicate acceptance, or you can use silence to signal your control of the interview. For example, you can use a pause or short silence to tell the interviewee that you expect more in response to a question.

Occasionally it is helpful to preface your questions in such a way that you lay a foundation the interviewee can use to consider the question (see Chapter 10 for a fuller discussion of this tactic); as in: "Now, Sam, even though you don't know for sure, you may have some suspicions about who is responsible here—possibly because of something someone said or did. Who comes to mind?" Having laid the foundation, pause and gently glance at the interviewee in an open expectant way. Wait for a reasonable time and look for indications that the interviewee is actively considering your request for information.

With the truthful interviewee, a furrowed brow, squinted eyes, and contemplative silence signal a mental search. All the while, they appear to be using some sort of mental cross-indexing in search of a key word that will lead them to where the data lies. The deceptive tend not to do this type of searching. Their mental file search is discernible but too quick.

Interviewees who resent your authority may engage in long intervals of silence before answering your questions (Davis). Whether or not they are resentful, some will use silence against you. So called street-sharp interviewees may sense that you are using silence as a tool and attempt to turn the tables on you. By being alert to the possibility of such game playing, you may avoid unnecessary conflicts with the interviewee and within yourself. Although the interviewee's silence may indeed make you uneasy, it is important not to suggest responses to your questions. An interviewee who realizes that silence makes you uncomfortable may intentionally use it in the interview to trap you into proceeding before your questions have been answered.

Even if an interviewee's silence makes you feel opposed or thwarted, it is vital that you not respond in an aggressive manner. Don't respond to the silence as though it were a personal attack on you (Benjamin). If there is no response to my question I will ask the same question in different words. This is not a time for harsh, piercing stares and tapping of fingers on the desk. I try to use silence as a warm waiting period allowing for clear thinking.

Because embarrassing silence is bothersome, I keep questions simple and direct, allowing the interviewee time to reply thoughtfully. Research "indicates that there is positive correlation between the amount of silence used by the interviewer and the respondent's general level of spontaneity" (Gorden, p. 188). When I pause between questions, interviewees often provide further information to fill the gap of silence. That silence often produces more meaningful and relevant information than a fast-moving interview (Drake).

Although there are times when what is happening during the interview shakes your confidence and impedes your thinking, develop positive ways of dealing with these mental shutdowns that can cause you to fall silent. It is important to hide the loss of your composure and train of thought. Interviewees can sense the implicit meaning of your silence and your consequent weakness. When this happens to you, and it probably will based on my experience, don't be surprised; take it in stride, try to regroup, and move on. Be ready; don't allow your mind to turn to mush.

Unless employed subtly, the interviewee may equate your silence with withdrawal and rejection. Silence unsettles interviewees when it occurs repeatedly. The silent treatment "is the ultimate form of rejection and a sure sign of displeasure" (Bennis et al., p. 78). Improperly used, your silence is a form of punishment and a self-defeating move; it offends the interviewee. Hence, abusive silence increases the interviewee's tension and discourages compliance. When you decide to use silence as a tactic, glance at the interviewee rather than stare. Staring can be oppressive. A strategic silence without a stare is enough to bring out meaningful existing tensions. Use silence to keep the pot bubbling, not to antagonize or alienate the interviewee. Silence can be a constructive part of your tactics and need not be a harsh method.

It is sometimes helpful to introduce silence when the interviewee least expects it. Note, however, that practiced interviewees can withstand silence. They handle it by sitting patiently or by asking questions intended to distract you from your inquiry. Some interviewees return the interviewer's stare with a calm, anticipatory look. The skill of interviewees in handling silence is a sign of their ability to handle distress. It is useful to try to gauge a given interviewee's ability in this regard. When I sense that interviewees are trying to employ silence to their advantage, I assume that they are also using other ploys to try to manipulate me. Formidable competitors, they need special attention, closer observation, and more careful assessment. When interviewees take too long to respond, I am neither in a hurry for the answer nor anxious to put words in their mouths.

Eye Contact

One of the most important nonverbal technique is the use of eye contact. Like gestures, eye contact works to control the flow of conversation. Most people look away for a few seconds before they finish speaking; they look back just as they conclude, signaling that it is the other person's turn to speak (Davis). Used properly, eye contact is effective in promoting rapport and establishing and maintaining communication.

You can learn a great deal about interviewees by the way they look, or fail to look, at you. As mentioned in Chapter 1, deceptive individuals often avoid direct eye contact; truthful interviewees usually make eye contact easily; and many people avoid eye contact when embarrassed or upset over a question. Use easy eye contact when interacting with everyone, and refrain from judgmental eye movements such as rolling your eyes upward in disbelief or disgust at an interviewee's comments. Remember that interviewees are looking for any sign that you are evaluating their behavior negatively. If you are a dominant, assertive individual, be careful how you use eye contact. Do not stare at the interviewee. You can observe as much with glances as you do by staring, but without alarming the interviewee about what judgments lie behind the stare. Be sure to allow the interviewee room in which to think clearly.

ESTABLISH RAPPORT

> "If thou art one to whom petition is made, be calm as thou listenest to what the petitioner has to say. Do not rebuff him before he has swept out his body or before he has said that for which he came. The petitioner likes attention to his words better than the fulfilling of that for which he came. . . . It is not necessary that everything about which he has petitioned should come to pass, but a good hearing is soothing to the heart."
>
> *Advice from father to son 5,000 years ago in* The Instruction of PTAH-HOTEP *and* The Instruction of KE'GEMNI, *p. 49. Translated by Battiscombe Gunn.*

This advice applies particularly well to investigative interviews and points the way to establishing rapport. Rapport is "an interpersonal relationship characterized by a spirit of cooperation, confidence and harmony" (Coleman, p. 750). In an interview, rapport is like an electric current that flows between participants. It is established in the very beginning of an interview, when you blend your verbal and nonverbal actions to those of the interviewee (Nirenberg) in active listening. The first few minutes are crucial: "Research has shown that people form their basic impressions of one another during the first few minutes of an interview" (Quinn and Zunin, pp. 8–14)

Building Rapport

Rapport is built on your ability to show that you are listening. Investigators who succeed in establishing rapport with interviewees during an interview demonstrate their empathy with the interviewee and generally obtain his or her truthful cooperation. Rapport does not require that the interviewer become emotionally involved or that the interviewer's commitment, persistence, and objectivity be eroded, merely that there be a psychological closeness (Davis).

Rapport involves "building a degree of comfortableness together, of trust in one another, and of basic goodwill that will permit non-defensive interaction. . . . You can build rapport through small talk, a good orientation, and a very warm, friendly manner" (Downs et al., pp. 57 and 201). Display expressions of genuine interest and empathy.

At the beginning of an interview, the interviewee may display signs of uneasiness. Naive investigators may think this unease is so obvious that they want to help the interviewee, surely the interviewee knows that the interviewer is trustworthy. Alas, this is not obvious, and the interviewer needs to build rapport in order to create trust. Try to project your trustworthiness to interviewees by showing that you understand and appreciate the speaker's feelings. Calm thinking and an atmosphere of open communication are vital. As rapport develops, you may notice a distinct sigh of relief, signaling a lessening of the interviewee's distress and the building of trust. From that point onward, the interview may take on a more relaxed character.

Sometimes, inexperienced investigators are so busy thinking up their next questions and trying to look prepared that they forget to listen to the interviewee's responses. They overlook creative opportunities to strengthen rapport. By the same token, investigators need to be alert to whether the interviewee is truly listening. Just because interviewees are silent and appear to be listening does not mean that they are truly receptive to what you are saying. They may be lost in an emotional maze of fear. Periodically ask questions designed to test whether the interviewee is listening. A blank unresponsive stare may signal distress, unclear thinking, or an unbalanced mental process.

Control your emotions without losing your enthusiasm. Keep your thoughts composed; think your comments through carefully before presenting them to the interviewee. Refuse to get ruffled; keep your goal clearly in mind. When interviewees discuss their problems and concerns, commiserate rather than suggest solutions. My experience suggests that when interviewees sense a closeness, they act more like trusting friends who will share hidden information. When I display insight into the person's life, the person tends to share information never shared before. The more rapport you can develop the more likely it is that you will hear information.

There are times when the first or second interaction does nothing more than establish a foundation. During a recent burglary investigation, I interviewed a man who seemed cooperative, but uneasy and restrained. The next day, he asked to talk with me again and during the second contact he provided helpful leads regarding a suspect. Many interviewees like to believe that they are in control, that they decide their own courses of action. If they sense that they are expected to decide to comply, interviewees may be approachable after they have had an opportunity to consider your request (Garrett). When interviewees know that they can leave the interview room if they choose, they often feel trust and faith in you (Bennis et al.). Their sense of freedom breaks down any fear that might hinder cooperation.

Diminishing Rapport

"Most people resist being thought of as inferior; therefore, they would be very reluctant to establish rapport with or to be persuaded by anyone who tries, consciously or unconsciously, to make them feel inferior" (Downs et al., p. 264). Actions that tend to block rapport include making negative comments, engaging in monologues, second-guessing the interviewee, displaying a condescending attitude, and trying to hurry through the interview (Downs et al.). Certainly, sarcasm, ridicule, or cynicism create tension that limits cooperation (Benjamin). Assist the interviewee to rationalize and save face.

Through role reversal an interviewee may skillfully unseat you and take over the role of leader in the interview. You become the interviewee providing information. An inexperienced investigator may not see the signals and may discover too late that he or she has given up command of the interview, answering rather than asking questions. This role reversal should be embarrassing only if it continues. Proficient interviewers realize when it is taking place and immediately regain control without making it too obvious or causing conflict. An interview is not the time for overt combat.

When leaving an unsuccessful interview, do nothing to create hard feelings. Even when hostile interviewees refuse to answer your questions, don't hold a grudge, show no frustration or anger, and don't allow yourself to vent your displeasure. Lay a positive foundation for future interviews. Leave all interviewees with a positive feeling, allowing them to believe they experienced a meaningful interaction.

CONCLUSION

Some interviewers feel they need to be assertive in interviews. They question the tactic of courteous neutrality and claim it is too ingratiating. In contrast, I have learned that no matter how terrible interviewees seem, they must be treated with the courtesy due all human beings if one expects cooperation. By treating the interviewee with respect, you are not trying to become his or her lifelong buddy, but to indirectly announce your acceptance of the interviewee and build rapport. You need to temporarily gain the interviewee's trust and break down his or her resistance so that you can obtain the testimonial evidence you need. Remember, your goal is to solve the case. If you expect more success and better results, you must modify your behavior accordingly.

REVIEW QUESTIONS

Answer the following questions and explain your answers fully.

Active Listening

1. Are interviews normal social encounters?
2. How is the interviewer a catalyst?
3. What are some characteristics of an active listener?
4. Can having good listening skills help you plan your strategy?

Acceptance

1. Why shouldn't you display your personal values?
2. What might your tolerance and indulgence signal to interviewees?

Concentration

1. What is a difference between mediocre and first-class interviewers?
2. What is involved in giving your undivided attention?
3. Is it important to concentrate during interviews?

Detachment

1. Is it important to be emotionally strong as an investigator?
2. What advantage is there to controlling you emotional actions?

3. How can you use the power of your will to control your behavior?

4. Can fear hinder cooperation?

5. What is an example of judgmental behavior?

Patience

1. How can you signal acceptance to the interviewee?

2. How might your boredom show?

3. How might you stimulate dialogue?

4. What are the advantages of treating each interviewee with decency and human dignity?

Nonverbal Active Listening

1. How is your whole body used in active listening?

2. How can you show that you are actively listening?

3. What is interactional synchrony and how can using synchrony help you during interviewing?

4. Can you use body language to signal positive messages?

5. How might nonverbals expose subconscious attitudes?

6. Can threatening silence strengthen rapport?

7. When interviewees are silent does that mean they are listening?

8. How can silence be used strategically and productively?

9. What is a form of ultimate rejection?

10. How might the resentful interviewee respond to your authority?

11. Does eye contact help control the flow of conversation?

12. Can a single negative message render an interview ineffective?

Rapport

1. What is rapport?

2. Is there some relationship between listening and rapport?

3. When should you start to establish rapport in the interview?

4. How might you go about building rapport?

5. Does your use of sarcasm, ridicule, or cynicism help you gain cooperation?

6. During the interview, what does the listener's blank look indicate?

7. Do you always gain cooperation during the first interview?

8. Is there ever a time to show your resentment over not gaining cooperation?

REFERENCES

Benjamin, Alfred. *The Helping Interview*. Boston: Houghton Mifflin, 1974.

Bennis, W.G., D.E. Berlew, E.H. Schein, and F.I. Steel. *Interpersonal Dynamics: Essays and Readings on Human Interaction, 3rd ed*. Homewood, IL: Dorsey Press, 1973.

Coleman, James C. *Abnormal Psychology and Modern Life, 5th ed*. Glenview, IL: Scott, Foresman, 1976.

Communication: *The Non-verbal Agenda*. Film. New York: McGraw-Hill Films, 1975.

Davis, Flora. *Inside Intuition*. New York: New American Library, Times Mirror, 1975.

Dexter, Lewis Anthony. *Elite and Specialized Interviewing*. Evanston, IL: Northwestern University Press, 1970.

Downs, Cal W., G. Paul Smeyak, and Ernest Martin. *Professional Interviewing*. New York: Harper and Row, 1980.

Drake, John D. *Interviewing for Managers: Sizing up People.* New York: American Management Association, 1972.

Garrett, Annette. *Interviewing: Its Principles and Methods.* New York: Family Service Association of America, 1972.

Gorden, Raymond L. *Interviewing Strategy, Techniques and Tactics.* Homewood, IL: Dorsey Press, 1969.

Gunn, Battiscombe. *The Instruction of PTAH-HOTEP and the Instruction of KE'GEMNI: The Oldest Books in the World.* West London: John Murray, 1918.

Keefe, William F. *Listen Management.* New York: McGraw-Hill, 1971.

Mallory, James D., Jr. *The Kink and I.* Wheaton, IL: Victor, 1977.

Nirenberg, Jesse S. *Getting through to People.* Englewood Cliffs, NJ: Prentice-Hall, 1963.

Quinn, L., and N. Zunin. *Contact: The First Four Minutes.* Los Angeles: Nash, 1972.

Scheflen, A.E. "Significance of Posture in Communications Systems." *Psychiatry 27/4* (November 1964).

Sherwood, Hugh. *The Journalistic Interview.* New York: Harper and Row, 1972.

Woody, Robert H. and Jane D. Woody, eds. *Clinical Assessment in Counseling and Psychotherapy.* New York: Appleton, Century, Crofts, Meredith, 1972.

Evidence

5

All clues, all traces of evidence are valuable when solving a crime. Even small bits of evidence may help prove someone's guilt, while limiting the search for evidence may lead to charging the wrong person with the crime. Therefore, the search for guilt or innocence arises out of the examination of all available evidence.

THREE TYPES OF EVIDENCE

There are three basic types of evidence: real (or tangible) evidence, documentary evidence, and testimonial evidence. Real and documentary evidence make up about 20 percent of all evidence introduced in courts of law. Testimonial evidence makes up the remaining 80 percent.

Real Evidence

Real, or physical, evidence is tangible. It is something you can put your hands on, pick up, photograph, chart, or store. It might be a bullet, a tire track, or a fingerprint. Real evidence is most often found at a crime scene and pertains directly to how the crime was committed and who is guilty. Such evidence is often fragile and fleeting. It requires expert handling if it is to be useful in court. When handling real evidence, the investigator must maintain a chain of custody, which records how the evidence was handled, in order to prove that it was not contaminated in any way.

Documentary Evidence

As indicated by its name, documentary evidence rests on a document of some kind. It includes such things as credit card receipts, hotel registers, and records maintained in the normal course of doing business. Documentary evidence is usually not found at a crime scene. Especially with crimes of passion, such as murder and assault, it is collected after the crime scene investigation has been completed.

In cases normally referred to as white-collar crimes like fraud or embezzlement, documents may be the only form of evidence; there are no tire tracks, blood drops, or shell casings. In these cases, investigators make a special effort to collect documents legally and quickly and to preserve them as evidence. Investigators need search warrants or subpoenas to obtain documents stored at a business.

The part played by documentary evidence in an investigation depends upon what is contained in the document. For example, information entered into a diary by a victim, witness, or suspect may be vital to the corroboration of certain issues. To verify that a person was a guest at a motel on a particular day, motel records and accounts for that date become important. Ownership of property may be recorded on a deed that bears an official stamp. Other such documents show proof of one kind or another to confirm or authenticate that a person was at a certain place or engaged in a specific activity.

THE CASE OF WAREHOUSE THEFT I

Documentary evidence might also be a videotape that shows someone committing a crime. In one case I investigated, several battery-powered drills, valued at about $200 each, were missing from a warehouse. I secretly installed video cameras in the warehouse in the hope of catching the thief in action. After several days, during which the cameras operated around the clock, another drill was reported missing. According to the company's records (another type of documentary evidence), it had not been sold. The videotape recorded at the time of the theft clearly revealed the thief, and I conducted an inquiry. Once the thief saw several still photos made from the videotape showing the theft in progress, he admitted his guilt and signed a confession. He obviously knew that the documentary evidence was overwhelming and could not be refuted.

Testimonial Evidence

Testimonial evidence consists of information provided orally by victims, witnesses, and suspects. It may subsequently be converted into written form. Interviews and interrogations are the main vehicles through which testimonial evidence is collected. Simply stated, the purpose of an interview is to collect truthful data on which future decisions and actions will be based. Some testimonial evidence consists of confessions investigators obtain by interrogating suspects.

An interrogation is a face-to-face meeting with a suspect with the distinct objective of obtaining an admission of guilt or confession in a violation of law, policy, or regulation. As a police officer and interviewer, you will gather this evidence. The more aware, the more observant, and the more interested you become in the process of interviewing, the better you can judge whether the evidence you gather is truthful.

VOLUNTARY CONFESSIONS

Rejection of a confession as evidence at trial is one penalty for failing to comply with certain basic legal requirements. A confession obtained after a "pickup" without probable cause (that is, reasonable grounds) to make an actual arrest cannot be used as evidence.[1] A confession must be voluntary before it will be acceptable as evidence. In their arguments against the admissibility of confessions in court, some defense attorneys claim that psychological coercion was used to obtain the confession. Arguments against using such coercion are explored throughout this book and specifically referred to in the Introduction.

At the beginning of an interview, seeking a confession from the interviewee is inappropriate. Instead, while treating the interviewee with compassion, simply try to uncover the truth and a confession may follow. To make sure a confession holds up in court, you must use the proper procedures when arranging the interrogation and during the interrogation itself. A suspect's voluntary response is vital. Make no illegal promises or threats while questioning a suspect. Law enforcement officers must make it clear that a suspect is not under arrest if that is the case. Be sure to make it clear to the suspect that he or she is free to leave if desired. If the inquiry is held in an official location, such as a police station, be sure that the interviewee knows whether or not he or she is being detained in custody.

MIRANDA WARNINGS

Before suspects "in police custody or otherwise deprived of freedom in any significant way"[2] can be interrogated, they must be apprised of their constitutional rights to remain silent and to confer with an attorney. In the 1966 case Miranda v. Arizona, the

Supreme Court held that the following warnings, known as the Miranda warnings, must be given:

1. A person has the right to remain silent and need not answer any questions.
2. If the person does answer questions, the answers can be used as evidence against him or her.
3. The person has a right to consult with a lawyer before or during questioning by the police.
4. If the person cannot afford to hire a lawyer, the state will provide one.

THE CASE OF BANK EMBEZZLEMENT I

In a bank embezzlement case I investigated, a teller (let's call her A) had shortages amounting to about $2,000 over a one-year period. I had the bank records searched to find out who had worked near the teller when the shortages occurred. The records showed that the same bank employee (whom we'll call B) had worked near A on all of the occasions when her money was missing. Using the interviewing process presented in this book, I became confident that B was not telling the truth about the missing money. In addition to stealing the missing $2,000 from her coworker's station, B also confessed to me that she had stolen another $5,000 that had mysteriously disappeared from a work table in the bank at the beginning of the year. Of that $5,000, about $2,700 was returned in the night depository with a note that read, "I think you may be able to use this." In all, B stated in her written, signed confession that she had stolen a total of $7,000 from the bank. The signed confession was documentary evidence of the theft. Because the confession stated that no threats or promises had been made to B at the time of her confession, the court determined that her confession was voluntary.

Delivering the Miranda Warnings

Miranda applies to "investigative custodial questioning aimed at eliciting evidence of a crime."[3] Be sure subjects in custody understand the Miranda warnings. You may not talk them out of refusing to talk once they have decided not to. If a subject wants a lawyer at any time, you may not attempt to change his or her mind. This ensures that subjects in custody know that they have the right to remain silent.

After receiving the required warnings and expressing a willingness to answer questions, a person in custody may legally answer your questions. Keep in mind that it is totally unnecessary to embellish or add new cautions to the Miranda warnings. Nor is it necessary to recite the content of the Miranda warnings using the precise language used by the court in drafting the Miranda ruling. The court require investigators to use advisement, not admonishment, in presenting the Miranda warnings.[4] In other words, it is necessary simply to tell the person in custody the content of the Miranda ruling. Merely expressing the warnings is sufficient; to do more is self-defeating. As you communicate the warnings, pay attention to your tone of voice and the message it carries. Stay neutral and straightforward. This is not the time to caution, advise, frighten, or admonish the person in custody. Do not sermonize about the Miranda warnings.

When the Miranda Warnings Are Required

In 1976 the Supreme Court removed the misconception that the warnings are to be given to anyone on whom suspicion is focused.[5] Rather, the warnings are required only when the subject is in police custody. In another case, the Supreme Court provided illustrations to define the meaning of "in police custody or otherwise deprived of freedom in any significant way." The Court said, "The key factors are the time of the interrogation, the number of officers involved, and the apparent formal arrest of the subject."[6] With reference to the questioning of a suspect not in custody within a police facility, the Supreme Court held in 1977 that:

> Any interview of one suspected of a crime by a police officer will have coercive aspects to it, simply by virtue of the fact that the police officer is part of a law enforcement system which may ultimately cause the suspect to be charged with a crime. But, police officers are not required to administer Miranda warnings to everyone whom they question. Nor is the requirement of warnings to be imposed simply because the questioning takes place in the station house, or because the questioned person is one whom the police suspect. Miranda warnings are required only where there has been such a restriction on a person's freedom as to render him 'in custody.' It was that sort of coercive environment to which Miranda by its terms was made applicable, and to which it is limited.[7]

Legally, interrogation is defined as asking a question, making a comment, displaying an object, or presenting a police report, if these actions call for a response that may be incriminating. Keep in mind that the subtle use of the aforementioned actions makes them functional equivalents of direct questions asked during an interrogation.[8] This means they, too, are bound by the Miranda warnings (although an exception can be found in Rhode Island v. Innes[9]).

If suspects who are not in custody freely consent to be interviewed or interrogated, there is no requirement that they be given the Miranda warnings. If an interviewee begins to confess, let him or her proceed without interruption to the conclusion of the confession. Immediately thereafter, give the Miranda warnings to prevent the court from holding that the interviewee entered custody at the conclusion of the confession and without the benefit of the Miranda safeguards. Custodial subjects may waive their constitutional rights. This is usually done in writing, but oral waivers will suffice.

TACTICS WHEN SEEKING A CONFESSION

It is vital to avoid saying or doing anything that might cause an innocent person to confess. Be fair and practical when interrogating anyone, particularly a suspect in custody. Consider the following legal tactics in an interrogation:

1. Exhibit your confident judgment that the subject committed, or shared in committing, the crime.
2. Present any circumstantial evidence to buttress your judgment and persuade the subject that denial is useless.
3. Watch the subject's behavior for indications of lying.
4. Empathize with and help the subject rationalize his or her participation and save face when talking about it.
5. Minimize the significance of the matter under investigation.
6. Offer nonjudgmental acceptance of the subject's behavior.
7. Encourage the subject to tell the truth.

Trickery

Trickery and deceit are often used in interrogations. The Supreme Court has given tacit recognition to the necessity of these tactics. In 1969, the Court held: "The fact that the police misrepresented the statements that [a suspected accomplice] had made is, while relevant, insufficient in our view to make this otherwise voluntary confession inadmissible. These cases must be decided by viewing the totality of the circumstances."[10]

Private Security Investigators

Police officers working private or part-time positions are still bound by the Miranda ruling. If you are not conducting the investigation as a police officer, the Miranda decision does not affect you unless you are acting in cooperation with the police as a police agent. It is important to realize, however, that regardless of your role as an investigator, if you compel someone to confess, you are coercing a confession that will not hold up as legal evidence. Even though private security investigators generally do not have to administer the Miranda warnings, they nonetheless should not abuse suspects.[11]

EVIDENCE PRESENTATION

Strict rules govern the handling of all evidence before it is presented in court. The court that ultimately hears the presentation of evidence will want to know if it was obtained legally, and who handled the evidence before it reached court. Does the evidence bear directly on the case and accurately represent what happened? Was it tampered with in any way? Is it tainted?

Finding and Collecting Evidence

What are you searching for? If the objective is to prove intent in a criminal, civil, or administrative investigation, you may be looking for documents bearing a certain date or signature. If it is a hit-and-run case, the evidence may be skid marks or the broken parts of a car. When interviewing an eyewitness, you may be searching for what the witness heard or saw at the crime scene. If a crime scene contains perishable evidence, such as blood or semen, quick and efficient action is necessary. A clear plan of action assigning qualified searchers to particular areas of the crime scene is effective.

Once you have located a piece of evidence, you must ensure that you will later be able to tell where you found it. Note the details of its location in the crime scene, and make sketches or take photographs. Your notes and written report covering these details will become important when presenting the evidence in court. If you obtained a confession, you will be challenged about how you obtained it. Did you determine that the suspect was lying based on your intuition and observations? If so, can you explain what verbal and or nonverbal signals caused you to conclude that the interviewee was lying?

As you collect evidence, you must make every effort to confirm that all evidence was obtained legally. This is done by following the rules of evidence prescribed by the court as defined in statutes and court rulings. These rules bear on real, documentary, and testimonial evidence. Regarding testimonial evidence, the main issue is whether or not the information was provided voluntarily.

Even though you may collect massive amounts of evidence, not all of it will be pertinent to your investigation. You may interview fifty people and find only two who have useful information. Details of the other forty-eight interviews need not play a significant role in your report other than references to the fact that you did conduct the interviews. Even hairs and fibers from a crime scene may not be relevant, but you will probably collect them anyway just in case they are important.

Preserving Evidence

All evidence, real, documentary, and testimonial, can become contaminated. When handling real evidence, it is especially important to use appropriately marked pillboxes and other containers to avoid contamination. Furthermore, it is important to provide a chain of custody describing the progressive locations and personal custody of the real evidence. For example, in the case of hair found at a crime scene, its specific location in the scene, who noticed it, and when, are important to determining if it has probative value later in a court of law. As far as a confession is concerned, courts consider who was present, what was said, and how it was said in deciding whether to admit a confession as evidence. If a confession is contaminated by the investigator's use of coercive tactics, threats, or illegal promises, then we can expect the court to throw it out. In addition, just saying that someone confessed to you, without producing a signed confession, will not usually stand up in court. Whenever possible, preserve confessions with any or all of the modern means available, such as video tape or tape recorder. At the very least, you should be able to present a hand-written statement signed and witnessed.

The chain of custody of any evidence will establish its credibility in court. Courts will typically ask for written reports about the collection of the evidence, its preservation, and relevant environmental factors that might bear on the reliability of the evidence. It is imperative that an investigator be able to show and verify that the evidence was not contaminated in any way before reaching court.

REPORT WRITING

Reports are official documents that detail how evidence was collected and preserved during investigations. The technique of reporting involves two basic qualities: a trained ability to observe, and fundamental communication skills. To be a competent investigator, you must write reports clearly so that everyone concerned will know what you did and why. Clear expression is not difficult to achieve, but it does take practice. The most important skill you can develop is to take full and complete notes and stick to the facts. Facts make up the backbone of all reports. A fact is something that can be verified and known as a certainty. Collecting facts is the basis of your work, and good notes are a prerequisite for a good report.

Well-written reports communicate better than sloppy reports and reflect positively on your education, your competence, and your professionalism. A report should give as full an account as possible of the facts it presents. Organize your information; report it in chronologically arranged paragraphs. Keep your writing straightforward and simple. Your reports show that you have done your job and that you recognize your responsibilities to the community you serve.

WRITTEN REPORTS

The Purpose of Written Reports

Reports are used to do the following:

- Examine the past.
- Keep other investigators informed.
- Continue investigations.
- Prepare court cases.
- Provide the court with relevant facts.
- Coordinate law enforcement activities.
- Plan for future law enforcement services.
- Evaluate law enforcement officers' performance.

The Basic Steps in Writing a Report

There are five basic steps in writing a report:

1. Gather the facts (investigate, interview, interrogate).
2. Record the facts immediately (take notes).
3. Organize the facts.
4. Write the report.
5. Evaluate the report (edit and proofread; revise if necessary).

Characteristics of a Well-Written Report

There are ten characteristics of a well-written report:

- Factual: It does not contain opinions, unless identified as such. When writing your reports, present your facts, draw your conclusions, and stipulate which is which. The who, what, when, and where questions should be answered by factual statements. The how and why questions may require inferences on your part. When this is the case, clearly label the statements as inferences or opinion. This is especially true when answering the question of motive. To avoid slanting the report, record all possible motives reported to you, no matter how implausible they may seem at the time.

- Accurate: It is specific. Use the past tense in reporting.
- Objective: It is fair and impartial. Keep in mind the necessity for precision, objectivity, accuracy, completeness, and brevity. Objective writing is disciplined, controlled, factual, and direct. Objectivity is one thing, and lack of clarity is another. Do not add or imply personal comments, even though subjective writing is more colorful than objective writing.
- Complete
- Concise: Make every word count—that is, eliminate unnecessary words, making reports more effective so that what you include in the report will be worded as concisely as possible; no one wants to read a wordy report. You can reduce wordiness two ways: (1) Leave out unnecessary information, and (2) use as few words as possible to record the necessary facts
- Clear

  - Your communication must be as clear and direct as possible.
  - Jargon creates confusion.
  - First-person writing. This is recommended for law enforcement reports because it is more direct.
  - Active voice. The active voice indicates what was done and who did it.

(continued)

- Include correct modification as details.
- Proper pronoun reference only to one person or object.
- Use parallelism—that is, use the same type of structure for similar parts of a sentence.
- Effective word choice—that is, do not use legal, technical, unfamiliar, or slang words. When you translate your ideas into words, follow the rules for correct writing. Just as there are rules for spelling, capitalization, and punctuation, there are rules for what words are used when. The words you choose must be broad enough to be inclusive and narrow enough to be exact. Accuracy and precision are much alike, but where precision deals with the selection of the specific word, accuracy deals with the selection of the correct word. A statement is the literal reproduction of the actual words spoken by the interviewee. You can assure objectivity in your reports by including all relevant facts and avoiding words with emotional overtones.
- Use specific, concrete facts and details.
- Keep descriptive words and phrases as close as possible to the words they describe.
- Use diagrams and sketches when a description is complex.

- Mechanically correct. Develop skill in spelling, capitalization, and punctuation. A mechanically poor report leaves a poor impression of its writer and what the writer did.
- Written in standard English.
- Legible.
- On time.

Source: Karen M. Hess and Henry M. Wrobleski, *For the Record: Report Writing in Law Enforcement*, Eureka, CA: Innovative Systems, 1988.

TESTIMONY IN COURTS OF LAW

The ultimate reason investigators collect and preserve testimonial evidence is to make that evidence available to the courts. Testimonial evidence is the foundation of both criminal and civil litigation and forms the basis for cross-examination. Evidence presented for consideration in court cannot intentionally be tainted. It cannot be tampered with and still be credible and trustworthy. True professionals maintain the integrity of the evidence and deserve society's respect.

Investigators are frequently called as expert witnesses to offer testimonial evidence in court. Those who have carried out their investigations honestly and carefully testify successfully. Investigators who are not called as expert witnesses are still obligated to tell the truth whether in court or when giving a legal deposition. "From the opposing attorney's point of view, the purpose of the deposition is to create a record for future impeachment. The deposition process can be a lengthy one. Be patient. . . . Hide your desire to get it over with. Show toughness and resolve and a willingness to stay as long as necessary" (Matson, Jack V., pages 41–42).

During a trial, attorneys often seek to impeach, meaning discredit, witnesses for the opposing side by challenging the truthfulness and consistency of their testimony. So be truthful, careful, and thorough. Maintain the integrity of the evidence. Gather facts and turn them into clear reports. By doing so, you will benefit the courts, and be a credit to your profession.

REVIEW QUESTIONS

Answer the following questions and explain your answers.

Three Types of Evidence

1. Identify three types of evidence, and give two examples of each.

2. What is the purpose of an interview?

3. What is the purpose of an interrogation?

Voluntary Confessions

1. Must a confession be voluntary?

2. What is a penalty for failing to comply with legal requirements? Why?

3. How can you avoid being impeached in court?

4. Why does the court reject some confessions?

Miranda Warnings

1. What are the four elements of the Miranda warnings?

2. When are you legally required to give the Miranda warnings? Discuss specific situations.

3. Name two differences between interviewing and interrogating.

Tactics When Seeking a Confession

1. Identify three or more legal interrogation tactics.

2. Is it okay to use trickery in trying to obtain a confession?

3. Is a confession legal if a private security person compels someone to confess?

Evidence Presentation

1. Why might psychological coercion preclude the admissibility of a confession in court?

2. Why is it important for the court to know the circumstances under which evidence is located, collected, preserved?

Report Writing

1. What is a fact?

2. What are the ten characteristics of a well-written report?

3. List the five basic steps in writing a report.

4. How can you ensure objectivity in your reports?

5. Why must communication in a report be clear and direct?

CASE CITATION NOTES

1. Dunaway v. New York, 442 U.S. 200, 99 S. Ct. 2248 (1979).

2. Miranda v. Arizona, 384 U.S. 436, 86 S. Ct. 1602 (1966).

3. Harryman v. Estelle, 616 F.2d 870 (5th Cir. 1980), pp. 881-82.

4. California v. Prysock, 453 U.S. 355, 101 S. Ct. 2806 (1981).

5. Beckwith v. United States, 425 U.S. 341, 96 S. Ct. 1612 (1976).

6. Orozco v. Texas, 394 U.S. 324, 89 S. Ct. 1095 (1969).

7. Oregon v. Mathiason, 429 U.S. 492, 97 S. Ct. 711 (1977).

8. Brewer v. Williams, 430 U.S. 387, 97 S. Ct. 1232 (1977).

9. Rhode Island v. Innes, 446 U.S. 291, 100 S. Ct. 1682 (1980).

10. Frazier v. Cupp, 394 U.S. 731, 89 S. Ct. 1420 (1969).

11. City of Grand Rapids v. Impens, 327 NW 2nd p. 278, 414 Michigan 667 (1982).

REFERENCES

Hess, Karen M., and Henry M. Wrobleski. *For the Record: Report Writing in Law Enforcement.* Eureka, CA: Innovative Systems, 1988.

Inbau, Fred, John Reid, and Joseph Buckley. *Criminal Interrogation and Confessions, 3rd ed.* Baltimore: Williams and Wilkins, 1986.

Matson, Jack V. *Effective Expert Witnessing.* Chelsea, MI: Lewis Publishers, Inc., 1990.

6

Public and Private Investigations

Whether from the private or public sectors, first-class investigators resemble each other more than they differ. They are successful because they share well-practiced skills, a high degree of perception, and positive attitudes. For the purposes of this chapter, we will define public investigators as official law enforcement agents, such as state or local police; and define private investigators as licensed private detectives or the internal security personnel of a company. While the number of investigators in the public sector has tended to remain relatively stable, the number of investigators in the private sector is growing as businesses decide to take more and more responsibility for the safety of their workers and goods.

Turf disputes of the past between public and private law enforcement have greatly diminished as progressive public sector leaders have joined with the American Society for Industrial Security (ASIS) in collaborative ventures to solve crimes. Together, they have changed their perspectives from antagonists to teammates who cooperate rather than compete. Although public and private sectors are distinctly separate legally, and there are certain legal restrictions which preclude the police from sharing particular information, where possible, more and more cooperation takes place. This chapter intends to review some distinctions between the kinds of crime private and public detectives investigate (with particular attention to white-collar crime), and the procedures they use.

THE UNIFORM CRIME REPORT

Before we continue, let's take a brief look at how crime is reported and classified in United States. City, county, and state law enforcement agencies keep track of the yearly incidence of different crimes in their jurisdictions. Compiled by volume and frequency, these statistics are sent to the FBI which issues the annual Uniform Crime Report (see Box). The FBI classifies the most serious, the most predatory crimes, under the heading, Part I Offenses. These crimes are most likely to be reported to the police, and therefore serve as the major index of crime in the United States. The crimes listed under Part II Offenses are considered less serious, less violent against individuals, and less damaging to the fabric of society. As you can see, fraud and embezzlement fall under Part II offenses, and we will return to this later.

INVESTIGATIONS

Clearly, the biggest difference between public and private investigators lies in the parameters within which each sector functions. Public investigators work within federal and state laws intended to protect citizens from the abuse of police power. In addition, police must work within the bureaucracy and operating procedures of their respective agencies. Certainly, private investigators also must obey the law, but because they set their own agendas, they have more independence. Large businesses frequently keep trained personnel on staff to investigate offenses ranging from stalking to theft. Typically, if a case involves a Part

I offense, the internal investigation is turned over to the appropriate police agency. If the case can be investigated by internal security personnel, it is. Private in-house investigators sometimes take investigative liberties that seem unreasonable, but their behavior is controlled by company policy, and is confined to company property. Furthermore, the company's and investigator's behavior are limited by the threat of a costly civil suit.

THE UNIFORM CRIME REPORT CLASSIFICATIONS

Part I Offenses	*Part II Offenses*
Murder	Other assaults
Rape	Forgery or counterfeiting
Robbery	Fraud
Aggravated assault	Embezzlement
Burglary	Stolen property (possession, and so forth)
Larceny	
Motor vehicle theft	Vandalism
Arson	Weapons (possession, and so forth)
	Prostitution
	Other sex offenses
	Narcotics
	Gambling
	Family/children (abuse, neglect, and so forth)
	Driving under the influence (DUI)
	Violation of liquor laws
	Disorderly conduct
	Other offenses

Traditionally, private investigators have dealt with fraud and embezzlement while the police have handled the violent crimes of murder, rape, and assault. Until recently, public investigators received no training in pursuing sophisticated white-collar crime. (We will return to the reasons for this later.) Rather, police training emphasized diffusing violent situations, coming to an individual's aid in a violent confrontation, shooting straight, and cardiopulmonary resuscitation (CPR). The subtle aspects of human interaction, the gentle art of communication, and their usefulness in investigative interviewing were all but ignored.

Rules of Evidence

Please look over Figure 6-1, and try to visualize which offenses might require the different types of evidence listed. Consider that each offense is covered by complex state and federal statutes. These laws define the offense in terms of specific behavior, the evidence required to prosecute the behavior, and the procedures to be followed in collecting the evidence and proving guilt.

A comprehensive review of how private and public investigators collect and present all the different kinds of evidence is beyond the scope of this book. Suffice it to say that federal and state laws limit how an investigation can be conducted and how evidence can be collected. This is true whether the investigator is a member of a large corporation's security staff, a hired private detective, or a police officer.

If a piece of evidence is to be of value to a corporation (or, for that matter, to society), and if I expect the evidence I collect as a private investigator to be accepted in criminal or civil courts, I must meet or exceed the standards set by the courts regarding collecting, transporting, and preserving evidence. This is true even when the evidence collected serves only to provide reasons for an employee's dismissal rather than prosecution in court. The case may turn ugly if the fired employee sues the company for wrongful termination and the company must produce the evidence on which it based the termination. If evidence collection

Figure 6-1.   Types of Evidence Associated with Various Offenses

and preservation fall short of acceptable standards, the company may be in deep trouble financially. In the public sector, of course, if a police investigator does not collect and preserve evidence properly, the prosecution may dissolve and the guilty party go free. Regardless of whether an offense is investigated by public or private detectives, the evidence needed to prosecute the case is the same.

Collecting Testimonial Evidence

Obviously, the main topic of this book is the collection of testimonial evidence through investigative interviewing. Most, if not all, offenses catalogued in the FBI's Uniform Crime Report require investigative interviewing of victims, witnesses, and suspects. Their testimonial evidence will one day arrive in court. As this book points out, the investigator's major job is to persuade the interviewee to cooperate—even if only for a short time—just long enough to reveal truthful information. To this end, investigators of all kinds must cultivate professional attitudes and techniques which will promote communication and cooperation.

While most interviewees will acquiesce to requests for information, they need encouragement from the investigator. There is always resistance to an investigator's inquiries. Some people believe that the degree of resistance depends on the nature of the offense under investigation. As covered in Chapter 2, however, I believe that the degree of resistance is a reflection of the interviewee's personality, the interviewer's attitude, and the qualities the interviewer can bring to bear on the interview. There is no blueprint for interviewing methods, although we are gradually formulating guidelines, of which this book is one example.

Are people more likely to refuse to cooperate with a private investigation than with a police investigation? Certainly people perceive less of a threat from private investigations. Realistically, most people consider loss of a job less damaging than being fined, going to jail, and losing a reputation. Still, employees are expected to cooperate in reasonable inquiries undertaken by company management. The refusal to cooperate in an investigation is often regarded by management as insubordination and sufficient cause for dismissal. But it does not prove that the employee is guilty. See "The Case of the Cussing Bank Teller" in the nearby box.

Occasionally the greater threat of a police investigation works against itself. Because of the fear a police interview can inspire, interviewees feel pressured to provide answers they sense the police want—and thus lead the police into wrongful arrest. During the 1980s, some police officers in Minnesota investigated charges of sexual molestation of children. Because of the interviewing tactics they used, some of the officers were sued. (They were later exonerated.) The court's opinion in that case (see box on the following page) shows how difficult it can be for police investigators to discover the truth while simultaneously protecting the rights of the alleged victims and the accused. It also highlights the need for comprehensive training in interviewing at the beginning, and throughout, a police officer's career.

THE CASE OF THE CUSSING BANK TELLER

In a bank embezzlement case, I was in the process of interviewing a teller when he refused to continue the interview. I had just explained that I believed there were some inconsistencies in what he had told me. He stood up and walked toward the door, saying loudly, "I'm not going to go through any more of this!" I said, "It's important that we continue this interview. I need to cover more information with you!" Still moving toward the door, he said, "I don't give a —— about your ——ing investigation!" With that, he walked out. Keep in mind that I had not yet begun an interrogation, though we were close to that point. I suspected him of embezzling the missing money, and I was beginning to edge into the interrogation to try to obtain an admission or a confession. He sensed where I was headed, and possibly because he had no answers to my accusation, ended the interview. Without hesitation, the bank's management ended his employment because he refused to cooperate. Note that the employee was not terminated because he stole the missing money. We had no proof of that; there was not enough evidence. The police were not called in about the missing money. The bank wrote off the loss.

REPORT ON SCOTT COUNTY INVESTIGATIONS BY MINNESOTA ATTORNEY GENERAL HUBERT H. HUMPHREY III.

In working with child sex abuse it is not unusual for children to initially deny being abused. In subsequent interviews they may finally admit what happened. However, the Scott County cases raise the issue of how long and how often one can continue to question children about abuse before running the risk of false accusation. While the record contains examples of investigative mistakes and flawed interrogation, particularly from the standpoint of successful prosecution of those implicated by children who have experienced extensive questioning, an imperfect investigation without more evidence does not deprive the investigators of qualified immunity. Immunity is forfeited for the questioning function upon at least a preliminary showing that the interrogation so exceeded clearly established legal norms for this function that reasonable persons in the detectives' position would have known their conduct was illegal. . . . We conclude that the interviewing conduct occurred in a gray area of investigative procedure [in which there are] less than clearly established legal norms. The gray area referred to involves the extent to which juvenile suspected victims may reasonably be questioned, particularly if they initially deny abuse, and the extent to which leading questions, confrontation with reports by others and photographs of suspects may be used. . . . We do not consider the standards for the interrogation of juvenile witnesses and victims, particularly in the area of sexual abuse, so clearly established in 1984 that on the basis of hindsight the deputies should now be forced to defend their questioning techniques in these damage suits.

TESTIMONIAL EVIDENCE IN WHITE-COLLAR CRIME
Embezzlement

Because of limited access to the inner workings of business, police agencies rarely know about the frauds and embezzlements that cause billions of dollars in loss across the United States. Many companies do not choose to advise the local police about these losses, but control them by establishing their own security or loss prevention staffs. Because embezzlement is a crime most often investigated privately, it offers a special window into the respective advantages and disadvantages of private and public investigations.

Federal guidelines define embezzlement as "the misappropriation or misapplication of money or property entrusted to one's care, custody, or control" (Uniform Crime Reports 1994, p. 383). Nationwide, billions of dollars are stolen through fraud and embezzlement from banking institutions. If the statistics are correct, then many states are being cheated of police attention to such crimes. As can be seen in the nearby box, in Minnesota alone, more than $400 million is stolen each year in white-collar crimes. (I choose statistics from Minnesota because it is a state with which I am familiar and because, like most states, it has not chosen to focus its police powers on white-collar crimes.)

At one time, the Federal Bureau of Investigation (FBI) investigated all internal bank thefts, and, technically, it still retains jurisdiction. But in reality, they do not investigate cases involving as minimal a loss as $2,000. It is just not cost effective unless truly large sums of money are involved. The Bureau has shifted its priorities, generally leaving local police agencies to investigate cases of fraud and embezzlement. Unfortunately, with few exceptions, local police officers have not been properly trained in such investigations.

Even if police personnel were properly trained to investigate embezzlement cases, the bank managers would probably not be comfortable calling them in. Based on my thirty years of experience, I am convinced that most businesses, banks in particular, do not want their internal problems made public. Many banks would rather not reveal incidents of internal theft because police reports draw embarrassing public attention to the bank's ability to keep the public's money safe.

Eventually a cycle develops which perpetuates local police departments' lack of familiarity with white-collar investigations. The cycle begins when businesses don't report embezzlement. Police departments, who build their statistics from reported crimes, continue to think embezzlement is an infrequent and relatively unimportant crime. Consequently, the departments don't train their officers to investigate it. When businesses do call in the police, the investigators don't understand the crime and mishandle the investigation. Business doesn't report the next incident, and the cycle continues. With proper training this cycle could interrupt, and police officers could handle such crimes for those

---

MINNESOTA CRIME INFORMATION, 1994.

Police agencies investigated a total of twelve embezzlement cases with the following results:

Sibley County Sheriff's Office: 1 case, solved.

Martin County Sheriff's Office: 1 case, solved.

Minneapolis Police Department, Hennepin County: 3 cases, 1 solved.

Redwing Police Department, Freeborn County: 1 case, not solved.

Bemidji Police Department, Beltrami County: 1 case, not solved.

Coon Rapids Police Department, Anoka County: 5 cases, 3 solved.

companies which do not have their own internal loss prevention department.

Police participation in embezzlement investigations promotes the public good. Where is that teller from "The Case of the Cussing Bank Teller" now? There is no police record on this suspected thief. The bank is not permitted to warn future employers about the teller's suspected role in the embezzlement, or even that he walked out during the investigation. If the police had been conducting the investigation, they would have made the teller's name part of the public record. The public would have had access to the police record once the investigation was complete, and prospective employers would have been able to research the teller's background.

Furthermore, had the police been involved, they could have used the tools at their command that are not available to private investigators—such as search warrants. If the bank had filed a civil suit to recover the missing money, it could have used subpoenas to obtain the teller's personal records and other documents that might have substantiated bank's case. From the bank's point of view, this type of lawsuit is difficult to prove without any testimonial evidence, and the bank had to weigh the public good against private damage. Since civil proceedings are generally open to the public, a loss of the bank's lawsuit would have added insult to the injury of bad publicity. Clearly, the bank thought it safer to handle the matter privately, and at least rid themselves of a damaging employee and stop the theft.

Two Cases of Embezzlement in the Private Sector

In "The Case of Bank Embezzlement II" (see following box), once again a bank called in a private investigator to solve an internal theft problem. In this instance, however, the theft was resolved with a confession. The major point here is that local police were not called in to solve the case because, "[they] don't know how to handle these things." Again, if local police had proper training they could indeed investigate such matters.

In contrast, "The Case of Cable Theft" (see box beginning on the next page) provides a model of public and private police cooperation. It demonstrates how the determination of the business owner caused the eventual prosecution of a delinquent employee, a thief. The illustrated theft is no small matter to business owners who are struggling to make ends meet. In this case, investigative interviewing provided the key to solving the thefts.

THE CASE OF BANK EMBEZZLEMENT II

Discrepancies had been noticed in the transactions of a young male teller. The teller was suspected of stealing $2,000 from the money he handled daily. His teller machine had been tampered with so that his work tape would not show the shortage. A teller machine is much like any cash register in a store; it produces a paper tape that the teller can review to check transactions throughout the day. Except this sophisticated instrument can do more, although, often, the tellers don't know or use the applications for overall bank operations and accounting purposes. The particular feature useful to my purposes was the ability to print out a comprehensive paper tape showing any and all manipulations of the teller machine. Attempts to hide the theft were foiled by a secret computer program that had recorded the real figures and showed how the teller, or someone else, had tried to hide the shortage. Fortunately, the bank that called me in on this case keeps close tabs on all aspects of their banking business as is required by the Federal Deposit Insurance Corporation (FDIC).

Before arriving at the bank to interview the suspect, I asked the bank security officer to print out the secret data showing the missing money. The teller and I met, and I asked him some basic questions—his name, date of birth, long he had worked at the bank. Then I gently announced, "I have looked over your teller tape, and I'm convinced that you walked off with $2,000 of the bank's money. Do you want to get this cleared up?" He agreed, and he and I put together a handwritten statement. He had needed the money to pay his bills.

The manipulated teller machine tape and the printout from the secret computer program became part of the documentary evidence. Because I was acting as the bank's agent during this inquiry, I had access to all pertinent bank data. The same information would have been available to the police, had they been called in. The handwritten statement provided further testimonial and documentary evidence.

THE CASE OF CABLE THEFT

Recently, a company that sells various cables asked me to conduct a private investigation into the internal theft of the company's product. Thousands of dollars' worth of cable had been stolen over the previous year. Two days before I was scheduled to visit the company to discuss the details, three spools of cable valued at $4,000 were stolen from the warehouse. I suggested that the company announce to its employees that an investigation of the losses would be undertaken. The night before I arrived, the three spools were clandestinely returned to the warehouse. The heat was on!

I interviewed several employees, one of whom seemed evasive in his verbal and nonverbal responses, which caused me to conclude that he was probably being deceptive. I did not seek any admissions from him, and I obtained none. Each of the six interviewees knew the value of the cable, had the opportunity to steal the spools, and had access to them when no

(continued)

one else was around. I was not ready to confront any of them yet, so I told each of them that I would speak to them again in the near future.

I then visited several scrap-metal yards within a fifty-mile radius of the company. An employee at one scrap yard verified that my main suspect had been selling pieces of cable as scrap for cash on numerous occasions. The transactions totaled several thousand dollars. Armed with copies of the scrap yard's records, I re-interviewed the suspected thief. After I reviewed the records with him and provided encouragement, he eventually admitted to stealing spools of cable, including the three that had been taken and returned shortly before my arrival. He signed a handwritten confession, a copy of which I submitted to the company. The thief lost his job that day. Sometime later, the local police contacted me for a statement regarding my part in solving the cable thefts and asked that I send the original signed statement to be used as evidence. The police investigator wanted to know the circumstances under which I obtained the confession in order to verify for the prosecutor that the confession had been voluntary.

This case involved both documentary and testimonial evidence. First, I collected documentary evidence to convince myself that the company had actually suffered the losses as it claimed. I collected more documentary evidence to show that the suspect had sold his employer's cable at the scrap yard. My written report of the investigation became more documentary evidence. I collected testimonial evidence in the form of an oral confession from the suspect. In written form, the signed confession became documentary evidence—a way to preserve the comments of the thief.

REVIEW QUESTIONS

Answer the following questions and explain your answers fully.

The Uniform Crime Report

1. What are some Part I offenses?
2. What are some Part II offenses?

Investigations

1. In what ways are private and public investigators alike?
2. What training do police officers mostly receive?
3. Is public law enforcement regulated more than private investigators when interviewing?
4. Are police officers properly trained in the investigation of such crimes as embezzlement?

Rules of Evidence

1. Which Part I and/or Part II offenses can be investigated without using interviewing or interrogating?
2. Does the private investigator have fewer requirements to meet than the police regarding the collection and preservation of evidence?

Collecting Testimonial Evidence

1. Is it usually necessary for the investigator to encourage interviewees to be cooperative?
2. What is the basis of interviewee compliance?

3. When might the risk of false accusations become a problem in sex abuse case investigations when interviewing children?

4. Are there legal norms for interviewing children?

Embezzlement

1. Define embezzlement.

2. Is white collar crime a significant problem in the United States?

3. Why do banks hesitate to reveal the thefts by employees?

4. Why do some companies not tell the police about their internal theft problems?

Cases

1. Do you think the teller in "The Case of the Cussing Bank Teller" case was thinking clearly?

2. What might the teller have done or said instead of walking out?

3. How was investigative interviewing important in "The Case of Cable Theft?"

4. How was investigative interviewing important in "The Bank Embezzlement Case?"

CASE CITATION NOTE

Attorney General Hubert H. Humphrey III, *Report on Scott County Investigations*, Feb. 12, 1985, p. 10. Library of Congress: HQ 72.U53 M64 1985, MN Attorney General, St. Paul, MN, 29 pages.

REFERENCES

Minnesota Crime Information 1994, prepared by: Minnesota Dept. of Public Safety, Bureau of Criminal Apprehension, St. Paul, MN, 55104.

Uniform Crime Reports for the United States, 1994, release date: November 19, 1995, printed annually by the Federal Bureau of Investigation, U.S. Department of Justice, Washington, D.C. 20535.

7

The Interview Process, Part I: Preparation and Contact

Thus far we have discussed tactical concepts. In this chapter we will start to pull them all together and make them more specific to the different stages of the interview. We will begin our overview of the essential stages of the interview process by looking at the first half of the process, the Historical, Personal Preparation, and Initial Phases. Chapter 8 continues this overview with the Primary, Terminal, and Follow-Up Phases. There is an interplay among all the stages during an interview, and the Polyphasic Flowchart shown in Figure 7–1 (Yeschke) illustrates all of the phases, approaches, and intensity levels encountered in an interview. These categories will take on more meaning as we proceed, but for now, allow the flowchart to serve as a road map of the interview process. Our goal is to acquire a stronger grasp on the application of the tactical concepts.

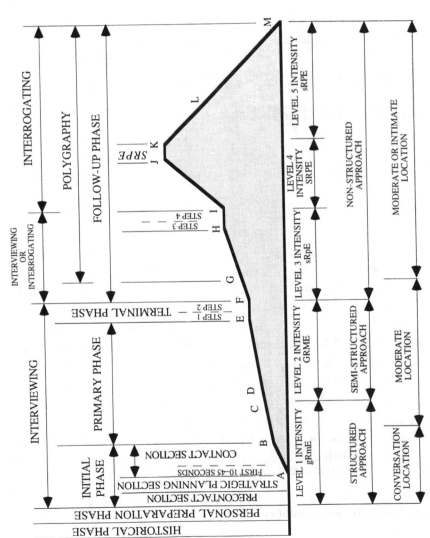

Figure 7-1. A Polyphasic Flowchart

THE HISTORICAL PHASE

The historical phase of the interview process begins long before investigator and interviewee ever meet. It covers all of the emotional and intellectual "baggage" we bring to the interview—attitudes and beliefs we learned in childhood and adulthood. We are conditioned directly or indirectly to approve or disapprove of others because of how they look, what they say, and how they act. Everyone's background determines how he or she views the self and others. What we see and hear is filtered through lenses built up over the years from what we have seen and heard before. In an effort to make sense of our world, we create categories from our childhood and adult experiences. We use these categories to interpret what we see or hear, quickly evaluating the appearances. For example, some of us put all men and women into two categories: men are either pimps or gentlemen; women are either whores or ladies. We learn who to hate in childhood, and some of us carry a great many negative attitudes in our emotional "baggage."

Undoubtedly, our emotional baggage influences and shapes our behavior during the interview process. Don't overlook or underestimate the importance of this phase. The more self-awareness you bring to the interview, the more effective you will be in the personal preparation phase.

THE PERSONAL PREPARATION PHASE

Biases and prejudices hamper our productivity and effectiveness. But we can control their influence. We can take on new behavior that is more suitable to a professional. In the personal preparation phase we set about modifying the contents of our emotional baggage. As mature adults in control of our own behavior we can take the opportunity to discard much of the garbage that clutters our thinking. Through education, training, and experience, we can modify our beliefs about others and thereby become more proficient investigators. We can know and accept that while many people are different from us, they still have worth as human beings.

As we have seen, biases and prejudice lead to misguided observation, evaluation, and assessment, so professionals don't knowingly bring them into inquiries. Still, investigators occasionally draw erroneous conclusions based upon prejudice, and accuse the wrong person of a crime. First-class investigators monitor their own thinking and behavior, remembering that just because a person is from a certain cultural background doesn't automatically mean that person is culpable. Professionals prevent such clouded judgment and miscalculation.

All investigators are not equally blessed in the way they handle human interactions. But all interviewers can be applied scientists, discriminating among variables and using systematic, purposeful investigative methods. Adapting to the differences in people helps investigators master their skills. Figure 7-2 provides another road map of the interview process, one that illustrates the thoughts and emotions behind the different stages. Note that in the personal preparation stage, you draw on your character, loyalty, and reputation to combat any negative attitudes lingering from your past. Investigators can develop humane skills and apply them in proficient ways. Their ethical behavior reveals itself as competence and leadership. Their capacities can build and their talents expand through practiced use. Investigators demonstrate their professional adaptability through their willingness to modify their behavior in a never-ending learning process.

THE INITIAL PHASE

The fundamental purpose of the Initial Phase of the interview process is to consider detailed information regarding the incident under investigation, the people who might be involved, and the conditions under which the interviews will take place. The Initial Phase consists of three sections: (1) Precontact, (2) Strategic Planning, and (3) Contact. The third section has to do with the

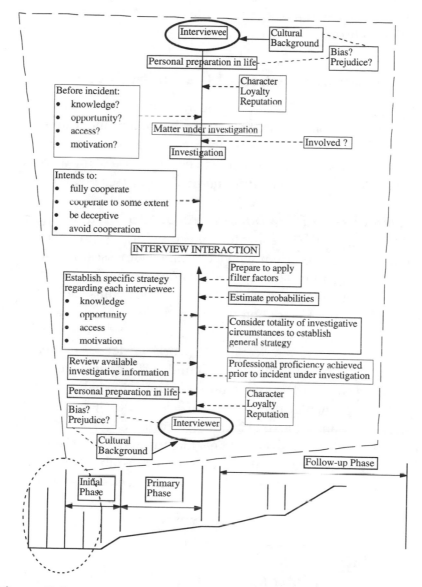

Figure 7-2. Elements Affecting Human Interaction in the Interview

first few critical minutes of each interview. We will discuss each section in turn.

The Precontact Section of the Initial Phase

During precontact (Figure 7-3), the interviewer becomes familiar with the available information about the matter under investigation and the various suspects, and begins to formulate a flexible interview plan. This plan includes a clear picture of the objectives of the interview and a floating-point strategy (see below).

Preliminary Inquiry During Precontact   During the precontact section, the investigator collects evidence and reviews information gathered from the victims and witnesses. The success of an investigation is often based on how thoroughly the investigator gathers this preliminary data. Specific details about the incident form the foundation to which the investigator will refer throughout the investigation. (These incident details may spur the investigator to dig deeper and work harder for evidence of culpability. Crimes such as sexual child abuse drive investigators to selfless efforts.) The investigator obtains information that suggests that particular people had sufficient knowledge, opportunity, access, and motive to commit the crime. An understanding of the interviewees' personalities, including habits and hobbies, is vital to effective, flexible planning. Clues about motivation may be found in the lifestyle, stresses, and needs of the suspects.

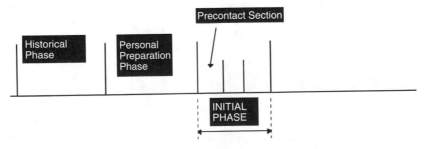

Figure 7-3.   The Precontact Section of the Initial Phase

The more you know about an interviewee, the more you can quickly build rapport and avoid topics that might make him or her defensive. For example, in one bank embezzlement investigation, I learned that the teller under suspicion was unmarried and had a young child. I used that information to commiserate about what must have seemed a justifiable reason to steal money. Just the fact that I knew of her having the young child allowed her the opportunity to rationalize taking the money for the child and not for some other less acceptable reason. My knowledge of her circumstances subtly indicated that I had taken the time to research and understand the pressures in her life.

Be careful when conducting the preliminary inquiry! A person who provides preliminary information in an investigation may have a hidden agenda—a plan to deceive and mislead you by providing false information. Be alert to all interviewees. Look for the telltale signs of deception: inconsistencies, illogical details, information clouded by fear or anger. Watch for calculated attempts to obscure the facts.

The Floating-Point Strategy   Investigations are often based upon probabilities and likelihoods. The investigator applies the floating-point strategy as soon as most of the elements of the investigation are known. The floating-point strategy is a flexible problem-solving process that can be used in all inquiries. Estimating the probability that a particular person committed the crime is the essence of the floating-point strategy. It allows the investigator to reevaluate and, if necessary, modify his or her operating hypothesis as new evidence is uncovered. With each new piece of evidence, a new sorting takes place: what to do next, whom to interview, where to place the point of your investigation. The point (or direction) of your inquiry will float (or change) as the inquiry develops.

Picture the problem-solving process as having numerous points at which you can evaluate your progress and determine if you are on the right track. Your strategy floats from evidence point to evidence point, never becoming fixed until you are reasonably sure in your assessment. My process of investigation swings from here to there as I learn more and more about the knowledge, opportunity, access, and motive of each possible suspect in the crime. For example, in one investigation, a guard was only one of many suspects in a bank theft. I learned that the bank guard had just returned from an expensive vacation with his girl friend and that he had recently purchased a new car. At this point it was possible that he was the thief. He had had a split-second opportunity to steal the missing money, and during his interview he gave me verbal and nonverbal signs of deception. It then became more probable that he was the thief. Finally, the guard requested a polygraph examination to verify his veracity. The examination showed indications of deception when he denied stealing the money. He subsequently confessed.

As you develop information about suspects, each person becomes the possible delinquent as you move from vantage point to vantage point in an effort to locate the truth of what happened. The payoff comes when you find an intellectual spot from which you can clearly see a path to the truth. An investigation is most often like a maze of passageways. Picture the investigator standing in that darkened maze looking for some light for guidance. With each question asked and answered a little more light shines on the path through the maze—the truth. Skillful investigators learn how to function in the darkness so that they don't stub their professional toes.

Strategic Planning Section of the Initial Phase

A novice interviewer may watch the casual performance of the experienced interviewer and wrongly assume that the relaxed interview atmosphere indicates no appreciable planning or research. The second part of the Initial Phase is the Strategic Planning section (Figure 7-4). During this part of the interview process, the investigator evaluates potential interviewees, prepares an interview strategy based on what he or she has learned, and prepares psychologically for the interview.

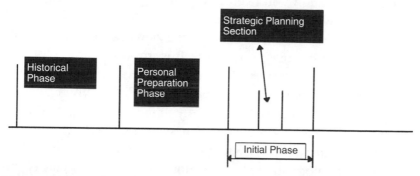

Figure 7-4.   Strategic Planning Section of the Initial Phase

Evaluating Potential Interviewees   Before conducting any interviews, the investigator evaluates each potential interviewee separately, based on information provided by those close to the investigation. The investigator then estimates the chances of obtaining truthful testimonial evidence from that person. This estimate is necessarily purely subjective—nothing more than thoughts about whether someone will be difficult or easy to interview—but the investigator uses this information to develop a strategy for each interview. As you prepare for an interview, you will probably need to evaluate potential interviewees sight unseen, based on the preliminary information you are given. You may have the opportunity to conduct background checks of potential interviewees and uncover strategic information that will allow you to predict whether or not they will cooperate—and why. Knowledge of an interviewee's cultural background can also help you understand him or her and counter any potential reluctance. Preparing for reluctance is vital, though you should always expect compliance

Preparing an Interview Strategy   The goal of an investigative interview is to gain as much truthful information as possible. You want interviewees to tell you everything they know about the matter under investigation. Interviewees hold the power of information, information you need to conclude the investigation successfully. As we have discussed, many factors (including your own attitude) determine whether interviewees decide to relinquish or hold onto this information. It is important, therefore, to plan an appropriate strategy for each interview, and it is better to be overprepared than underprepared, especially when dealing with people who may try to deceive you (Quinn and Zunin). Experienced interviewers make it look easy, but it's not. Author Eric Berne helps clarify the growth from the amateur to the professional. "The analogy in the field of motor activity helps clarify the point. A beginner dances the rumba by remembering to put one foot here, then one foot here, and so on, and by this additive process he gets along in an awkward way. After a while he no longer needs to remember, and as a result he dances a smooth, well-integrated rumba without thinking about it. If he is called upon to explain how he does it, however, he reverts to his former system temporarily" (Berne, p. 47). With each investigative experience, successful or not, the investigator builds capacities to handle the next investigative challenge.

Before conducting an interview, plan how you will behave during the encounter. How will you speak, and how will you act? How will you show energy, strength, and concentration? To what extent will you review details with the interviewee? Will your review of case details and circumstances with the interviewee help him or her remember additional information? How will you encourage him or her to be truthful? We will discuss encouragement and intensity in more depth in Chapter 9; in the meantime, just know that it is in the Planning Strategy section of the Initial Phase where you begin to anticipate how the interview will progress.

Preparing Psychologically for the Interview   Plan to enter an interview with an open mind. This means not only keeping your mind open to the guilt or innocence of each suspect, but being accepting and nonjudgmental, even when you will be interacting with those whom you have designated prime suspects. Review the discussion of human needs in Chapter 1, and positive attitudes in Chapter 2. Remember especially the self-fulfilling prophecy we discussed in Chapter 3, and the benefits of positive expectation. Use it in all your efforts to gather information. In everything you do and say, act as though you know the interviewee truly wants to cooperate with the investigation. In addition, reserve judgment about the worth of various pieces of information. I have frequently encountered well-meaning individuals who, unintentionally, offered misinformation. Be determined to put misinformation aside and think for yourself. Don't fasten onto any piece of information until you evaluate it in light of all the other evidence.

The Contact Section of the Initial Phase

Points A and B of Figure 7-5 define the first four minutes of the actual interview. I call this span of time the Contact Section of the Initial Phase. Your main purpose during these first four minutes is to establish a rapport (see Chapter 4). Building rapport with the subject is critical to the success of the interview and a major accomplishment. Also during this section you begin to use the tactics referred to as filter factors. These first four minutes set the stage for the balance of the interview, and, in addition, serve as the potential beginning of an interrogation in the Follow-Up Phase (see the Polyphasic Flowchart in Figure 7-1).

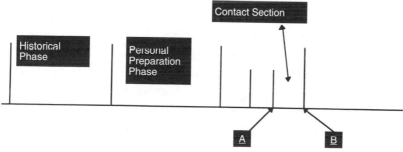

Figure 7-5.   The Contact Section of the Initial Phase

Using Filter Factors Throughout your career, you will learn to use certain tactics when gathering information during an interview. For example, you will learn to build rapport with the interviewee, to maintain a positive attitude, and to listen actively. These tactics, which I call "filter factors," will—if used sensitively and skillfully—have significant and positive effects on the outcome of your interviews. I call them filter factors because they help the interviewer display favorable characteristics and screen out less favorable ones. They are designed to show the interviewee that the interviewer can be trusted. In most interviews, the investigator has at least one hidden agenda, some unannounced reason for conducting the interview. For example, one hidden agenda when interviewing a victim is to determine if a crime actually took place. While the victim may think that you are only seeking details, and you are, at the same time you are watching for any signs of fabrication.

In one of my investigations, the female manager of a convenience store reported being taken by force in her van to a secluded part of town after she was surprised by a thief who had been hiding in the back of her van. The thief assaulted her as she drove to the bank one evening with about $3,000.00 of receipts from the store. She claimed the thief ordered her to drive to a parking area and forced her to walk with him down toward a lake where he told her to stand while he drove away in her van. But it had been snowing and there was only one pair of shoe prints in the snow. Confronted with the inconsistencies of her story, she confessed stealing the money to pay family bills. She had hidden portions of the stolen money in the rafters of her garage where police detectives found it.

Practiced use of the filter factors can help the interviewer keep the hidden agenda hidden. During the first few minutes of the interview, begin using the filter factors that follow, and continue using them during the Primary Phase and even into the Follow-Up. These filter factors are:

- Consider the human needs of interview participants.
- Continue to build and maintain rapport.

- Apply flexible methods.
- Cover suspiciousness.
- Use creative imagination.
- Apply the Self-Fulfilling Prophecy.
- Exhibit human warmth, sensitivity, empathy, respect, and genuineness.
- Use nonjudgmental acceptance.
- Cover personal values.
- Use active, attentive listening.
- Be patient.
- Be "positive": Use positive silence, positive eye contact, positive proximics, positive kinesics, and use positive haptics where appropriate.
- Maintain a positive, neutral stance.
- Maintain a positive attitude.
- Use positive power and positive control.
- Control personal anger—avoid antagonizing or harassing interviewees.
- Avoid using coercive behavior.
- Use observation, evaluation, and assessment.
- Avoid using the third degree.
- Use closed questions and open questions when appropriate.
- Keep your questions simple and avoid using double-meaning questions.
- Dare to ask tough questions.
- Use unasked questions (assume answered yes).
- Properly use leading questions, and use self-appraisal questions.
- Handle trial-balloon questions.
- Finally, always assume more data is available.

Making First Impressions Count   During the first 10 to 45 seconds of an interview you make your first impression and you never get a second chance. With a pleasant tone of voice and warm eye contact, act calm and friendly. Using the attentive listening techniques we discussed in Chapter 4, be firm, fair, and compassionate. In other words, be professional—the opposite of rude, abrasive, and condescending. Although face-to-face interviews are preferred, in a telephone interview, you can express these qualities through your tone of voice, timing, and silences. Your strategy should incorporate the awareness that some people are more than ready to tell the truth. Because I treat suspects as though they are ready, willing, and able to tell me the truth, it does not surprise me when someone does. I expect it to happen. Even confessions need not be a surprise. Be especially braced against jumping for joy when you get an admission of guilt. I have had numerous situations in which suspects, without any specific encouragement from me, volunteered confessions during the first few minutes of an interview. Take it all in stride and maintain your professional style.

The Interviewee's Evaluation Process   You can expect the interviewee to start an evaluation process with his or her first glimpse of you. How do you look? Do you appear to be a professional? How do you sound? Do you seem overbearing? In those first minutes, the interviewee senses whether you are biased or neutral in your collection of facts. Consciously or unconsciously even the slowest, least educated interviewees evaluate you to decide whether it is safe to reveal information or whether they will be abused in the process. If there is a time to open the door to the truth, it is in these first four minutes when the interviewee is deciding whether it is safe to speak with you. Remember that your tone of voice, choice of words, and gestures express particular attitudes. This is the time to signal that you want the interview to be a friendly interaction. Subsequent interviewees will evaluate the interview process, in part, based on how you treated preceding interviewees. The message about you and your methods will be conveyed to everyone in an undertone—that you are okay or not, fair or not, biased or not.

There is some strategic advantage if the interviewee is not under arrest when interviewed; faced with less of a threat, there is less distress and cooperation is more likely. Although the interviewee may still be uncomfortable, your professional demeanor and friendly ways will make you the suitable recipient of important information. You want to send the subtle message that talking to you is beneficial, propitious, and agreeable.

Interviewees continue evaluating throughout the interaction. Be ready to modify your words and actions as you evaluate the interviewee feedback. Both participants are shifting, adapting, and presenting themselves and their information as their intuition guides them during the interview (see the discussion of intuition in Chapter 2).

Elements of the Contact Section

Introduction and Greeting   A formal introduction will help establish you as someone in whom it is safe to confide. Introductions vary depending on the situation. Most recently, I interviewed nineteen employees of a company which had been burglarized and suffered a loss of about $3,000. The introduction in this case consisted of a company memorandum which announced that the company was undertaking a private inquiry into the recent burglary. It clearly stated that a private investigator had been hired to interview employees. Their cooperation was requested and my name and phone number were provided if they wanted to contact me away from company property.

Interviews were scheduled according to employee availability and work schedule. When each interviewee arrived at the interview site, I said: "Hello, my name is Charles Yeschke. Would you have a seat there, please [motioning to a chair]. I'm a private investigator looking into the theft that took place here recently. I'm asking everyone the same basic questions. If you will please share with me as we go along, I want to cover some areas with you on that break-in." In this illustration, two types of introduction greeted the employee: the memo and my comments.

In another investigation of bank embezzlement, each interviewee was introduced to me by the bank security officer as the interviewee entered the interview room. Such individual introductions can become too formal, too stiff, and may unfavorably affect your effort to build rapport. In this case, I felt it necessary to tell the bank representative not to make the introductions but to merely tell the employees that they were to be interviewed and who was conducting the interviews. The security person escorted each interviewee to the interview room, but didn't enter, and I then introduced myself.

During the first few minutes, the tone of the interview is determined, and it may last for minutes, hours, or days. If the interviewee offers to shake hands when we meet, then I do, but I don't routinely offer a handshake to each interviewee. I usually try to remain professionally aloof to signal the serious nature of the inquiry. I try to appear reserved, not stuffy. Generally, I feel that small talk is not appropriate, and I avoid all forms of intimidation and abusiveness that might in any way spark resentment or defensiveness. I want victims, witnesses, and suspects alike to feel free to talk to me.

When possible, it is useful to separate yourself from any prior investigations of the crime you are asked to solve. You want to appear to be a fresh face, unbiased, uncontaminated by the actions of others. I have entered many investigations during the past thirty years which were considered almost irredeemably lost to resolution. I was brought in to solve the case or bury it. If you are independent and insulated from political pressure, you will probably gain the trust of those who hold vital evidence. When people realize that you will conduct a truly professional inquiry, they will probably cooperate.

Seating   For the interview, choose a location that provides both privacy and comfort. Determine the seating arrangements in advance. When possible, I arrange the chairs so that the interviewee and I will face one another across a space of about six to eight feet and there will be an uncluttered wall behind me. As the interview progresses, I usually move my chair to within about four feet of the interviewee. I try to use chairs of similar design and comfort. Obviously, chairs and their location are a ridiculous consideration at an accident scene, but the important point is not to move too quickly into the interviewee's personal space (more about this in Chapter 9).

Announcing Your Objective   Announce the objective of the interview in answer to the interviewee's usually unasked query about why he or she is being questioned. Tell the interviewee that you want to determine how the incident you're investigating happened; that you want to prevent similar events in the future. For example, you might say: "The purpose of our talk today is to discuss the building materials that are missing from the warehouse. I'm looking for information that will help me determine how the materials were removed so that I can make clear recommendations to prevent another disappearance in the future. I'm interviewing several people, and I need your assistance to get a better view of the circumstances. First, let me get a little background data about you so that I can get to know you a little better." Never announce your objective as identifying and prosecuting the guilty party. This produces too much fear and blocks cooperation in the guilty and non-guilty alike. When beginning an interview, adopt an open manner that invites the interviewee to share any thoughts, observations, opinions, or facts that may have a bearing on the crime. This invitation should be implied, not actually spoken, and you should show appreciation for the cooperation when it comes.

Setting the Tone   After you have announced the objective and during those critical first few minutes of the interaction, ask the interviewee questions that will be easy to answer: the spelling of his or her name, date of birth, number of years of employment, current position, years of education, marital status. These questions give the interviewee the opportunity to vent some emotional energy and feel more comfortable. At this stage of the investigation, you may note evasiveness and lack of cooperation. Try to determine if the interviewee is signaling fear or deception. Adapt to the interviewee's feedback and use a toned down style to avoid any suggestion of intense confrontation. Too often, investigators, believing they will quickly unmask the guilty party, interrogate every interviewee in a prosecutorial manner. I see no justification for a confrontational style in the Initial Phase. I avoid using quick questions and burning stares. At the outset of each interview my choice of words and phrases is intended to exhibit my positive attitude and expectations.

Contact at the Crime Scene   At a crime scene the victim's fear is so immediate and powerful that it cannot be dissipated by the victim's exercise of self-control alone. Your help in reducing a victim's fear becomes paramount. An investigator's hurried approach will only cause confusion and heighten distress. Be patient and calm; reassure the victim by saying something like, "You're safe now." Showing proper regard for the victim's feelings builds empathy which facilitates questioning and produces accurate recollections. At a crime scene, you should locate witnesses, identify yourself, explain the reason for the contact, and record their names. Establish their credibility by making sure they could in fact see and hear what they report. It is indispensable that you give the interviewee your full attention. Judicious eye contact is an effective way to establish and maintain communication. Effective interviewers encourage an interviewee to provide a narrative account of his or her observations of the incident under investigation. Ask witnesses to recollect everything observed. Speak slowly, softly, and firmly to show that you are capable of both comprehending and solving the investigation. Rather than use rapid-fire questions, allow the interviewee time to answer fully without interruption. Then ask more specific questions to add details. All the while, take notes and be attentive.

The quality of information gained depends upon the interviewer's interpersonal communication skills. While many interviewees are impartial and willing to relate what they know, others fear contact with legal authorities. Still others are affected by physical and emotional factors that distort their perceptions and the reliability of their information. Some interviewees may not want to become involved in the investigation because they distrust the legal system. For other interviewees, the time and energy involved in giving testimony at a trial seem an unnecessary burden. An investigator needs to see all of these reluctant witnesses as presenting a challenge to his ability to build rapport and establish genuine communication.

Once an interviewee's narrative account has been presented, it is vital to review and summarize details to ensure the report is complete. The plausibility of witness observation is critical to the overall investigation. Be careful not to contaminate the witness's information by suggesting what you specifically want to hear. It is not appropriate to use leading questions such as, "You saw the tall guy carry a gun in his right hand, didn't you?" or, "The little guy didn't have much chance to get away, so he shot the tall guy, right?" Weak interviewees may parrot your words back to you rather than tell you what they actually saw and heard.

Because of the urgency of some criminal investigations, it is not always possible to prepare fully for an interview. In such a situation, gather basic information immediately; later, in a recontact interview, obtain additional facts under more favorable conditions. Remember, however, that the greater the time lapse between the incident and the interview of witnesses, the less chance there is that they will be able to report accurately what they observed. Furthermore, they may be reluctant to cooperate fully once the excitement of the incident has subsided and they have discussed it with others. People tend to seek group consensus, and they will often adopt the group opinion as their own regardless of whether they believe it to be correct. If not separated quickly and interviewed, witnesses may compare stories and adopt parts of the accounts of others at the crime scene. Fear of reprisal may intimidate interviewees so much that they refuse to cooperate. Therefore, identify victims and witnesses quickly, and interview them at some distance, if not a separate location, from the suspects. Make a special point of interviewing alibi witnesses promptly to reduce the possibility that suspect and witness will take the opportunity to corroborate their stories and cover up the suspect's participation in the crime.

REVIEW QUESTIONS

Answer the following questions and explain your answers fully.

The Historical and Personal Preparation Phases

1. How and when do we learn bias and prejudice?

2. Who is in charge of changing our attitudes as we mature and how does it happen?

3. How can you build your capacity as an investigator?

4. Does your learning process ever end?

5. Is it possible for you to take on new behavior?

The Initial Phase

1. What are the three sections of the Initial Phase?

2. Explain the Precontact Section.

3. What is the Floating-Point Strategy?

4. How does the Floating-Point Strategy aid the problem-solving process?

5. Can the success of the investigation be influenced by information?

The Strategic Planning Section

1. What is meant by estimating probability when setting up an interview plan?

2. Does it help you to know the cultural background of an interviewee?

3. What is the goal of an investigative interview?

4. Is it better to be overprepared for an interview?

5. What is the impact of your courage, spirit, and confidence upon the interviewee?

6. What does it mean to have an open mind as an interviewer?

7. What does it mean to have positive expectations?

The Contact Section

1. What is the main purpose of the first four minutes of an interview?

2. What are filter factors in interviewing?

3. Is having a hidden agenda unusual during an interview?

4. How can you be ready for an interviewee to confess immediately?

5. Does the interviewee evaluate the investigator in any way?

6. What is the strategic advantage in interviewing someone who is not under arrest?

7. Why does it help you to have friendly way when interviewing?

8. Is a formal introduction necessary in each interview?

9. How might the objective of the interview be mentioned to the interviewee?

10. What can the interviewer do to promote interviewee comfort and thought?

11. How do interpersonal communication skills help the interviewer?

12. How does interviewee fear impact the interview process?

13. What are some reasons a person may not want to become involved in the investigation?

REFERENCES

Berne, Eric. *Intuition and Ego States*. San Francisco: TA Press, 1977.

Dougherty, George S. *The Criminal as a Human Being*. New York: Appleton, 1924.

Quinn, L., and N. Zunin. *Contact: The First Four Minutes*. Los Angeles: Nash, 1972.

Yeschke, Charles L. *Interviewing: A Forensic Guide to Interrogation*, 2nd ed. Springfield, IL: Charles C Thomas, 1993.

8

The Interview Process, Part II: Evaluation and Closure

In this chapter, we continue our discussion of the interview process with the remaining three phases: the Primary Phase, the Terminal Phase, and the Follow-Up Phase. You may find it helpful to refer once again to our interview "road map" shown in the Polyphasic Flowchart of Figure 7-1. We begin our discussion with the Primary Phase.

THE PRIMARY PHASE OF THE INTERVIEW PROCESS

The Primary Phase follows the Contact Section of the Initial Phase as the interview process continues. On the flowchart shown in Figure 8-1, it begins at point B after about the first four minutes of the actual interview. The purpose of the primary phase is to allow the interviewer to strengthen the rapport begun

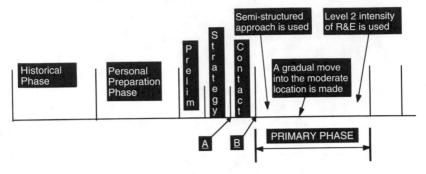

Figure 8-1. The Primary Phase, Showing Approach, Location, and Intensity

in the Contact Section, gather more information through active listening, and watch for signs of deception.

Overview

By point B, the investigator has gathered information in the Preliminary Inquiry Section, and has made an educated guess about what happened and who did it. Working with this hypothesis and following the path laid out during the Strategic Planning Section, the interviewer has prepared to use the floating-point strategy as he or she moves from interviewee to interviewee. Throughout the Primary Phase the interviewer tests the hypothesis as more details are learned and inconsistencies appear and resolve. Frequently some resolution leads the investigator to a conclusion, at which point he or she and moves on into the Terminal and Follow-Up phases.

In the Primary Phase the investigator asks questions and presents alternative scenarios, then awaits the interviewee's verbal and nonverbal responses. Since deceptive and truthful interviewees generally tend to respond differently, a particular interviewee's responses form a pattern. We might call the Primary Phase the "Bait and Bite" phase—deceptive interviewees take a big bite of the bait, the truthful don't even nibble. By pay-

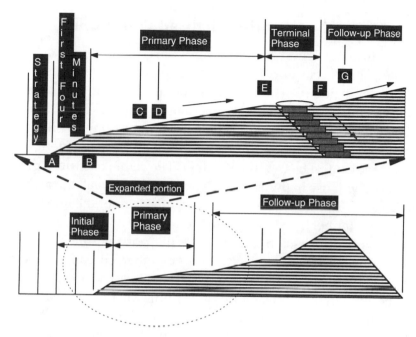

Figure 8-2. The Primary Phase

ing close attention, the interviewer does the major work of evaluating an interviewee's testimony in this phase.

At the beginning of the Primary Phase the interviewer gradually moves his or her chair closer to the interviewee (the moderate location discussed in more detail in Chapter 9). Between points B and C in the diagram, the investigator reviews the case information with the interviewee as a prelude to asking additional questions. All the while, he or she tries to reinforce a positive tone in the interaction and build rapport. Exactly how you will proceed, which questions you will ask, and how you will formulate them, depends as much on the quality of the interaction you have been able to establish as on the facts you still need to gather. The investigator's adaptability is vital. Remaining imaginative and creative is far more important than following a regimented design. (See Chapter 10 for more on question formulation.)

The "Bones" or Semi-Structured Questions

Around points C and D on the flowchart, I use what I call the "bones," non-accusatory questions that reveal the elements of the complete incident. These semi-structured questions operate much as the bones of the body make up a whole skeleton. In the same way that muscle and tissue surround our bones, all of the details of the incident and the interviewee's involvement surround the central facts of the incident. The semi-structured questions you will use in this phase are designed to reveal, through an interviewee's pattern of responses, whether or not the interviewee is lying (either by commission or omission) or telling the truth. Move with compassion and employ the positive filters. Avoid hasty conclusions and accusations. Remember, culpable individuals are understandably reluctant to reveal a truth that brings shame, embarrassment, and possible punishment. As a lead-in to using the semi-structured questions, you might say, "As I mentioned before, I'm trying to determine how the loss happened. So, let me ask you a few questions." Then proceed with the following series of questions.

The "What Happened" Question, Narration   Early on in the Primary Phase of the interview is the logical point to ask the interviewee to tell you what happened—what they know about the incident under investigation. Truthful interviewees tend to provide smooth-flowing narratives that have been clearly thought out; they may offer suggestions to help you solve the matter. Untruthful interviewees must weigh everything they say, and gaps appear in their narrations.

The "You" Question   Address the interviewee by name, and begin this question by saying, "It's important to get this matter cleared up." Briefly review the reported incident, and say that you are asking these questions in an effort to determine what happened and who did it. It's a direct question that opens, and serves as a foundation for, a full discussion of the incident. The "You" question might take several forms. Here are a few examples:

- "John, if you're the one who took the money, it's important to get it cleared up. How do you stand on this? Did you take the money?"
- "The report claims that you had contact with Rita. If you did, it's important to get this straightened out and clear things up. So, Sam, let me ask, did you have any contact with Rita?"

Note the use of the conditional word "if" to soften the impact of this question. While rare at this point, occasionally, if an interviewee has a high level of shame and remorse, he or she cannot stand the stress of an investigation and provides a full confession. Do not ask this question accusingly, but with a positive tone of open curiosity. "If the interviewee is hiding something, your genuine curiosity will provoke unease and evasion exhibited by such outward signs as squirming and preening. Such signs of evasion and possible deception may take place in about a hundredth of a second. You must be attentive to notice these signals without being obvious" (Yeschke, p. 93).

The "Who" and "Suspicion" Questions   These questions work together as the first sets up the second. You might begin with a preamble, such as, "Knowing for sure who did set the fire in the warehouse is one thing, but having suspicions is something else. Do you know for sure who set the fire?" The interviewee will probably respond negatively, which leads nicely into the next question. "Okay, you don't know for sure who did it, but let me ask you, do you have any suspicions of who may have set the fire?" Quickly add the caveat, "Keep in mind that I'm not asking you to be malicious, to arbitrarily point a finger at someone, because that wouldn't be fair. I'm just wondering if anyone has done anything or said anything to cause you to think they may have set the fire. Can you think of anyone?" Typical responses from honest interviewees include, "I can't imagine who did it or why" or, "If one of my coworkers did it, he'd have to be a Jekyll-and-Hyde personality."

The "Trust" Question   This question usually takes the form, "Who comes to mind that you trust? Who, do you think, could not possibly have stolen the computer equipment?" or, "Of all the people that had the opportunity, who, do you think, would not have embezzled the money?" The blameless tend to specifically name those trusted, while the culpable are unwilling to name anyone specifically.

The "Verification-of-the-Incident" Question   "After considering the situation, do you think the money was really stolen, or do you think the theft report is false?" The culpable may say they don't think the loss was caused by theft. "It must have been a mistake or misplaced in some way." The blameless tend to acknowledge the report as correct, saying the theft was real.

The "Approach" Question   "Life presents many temptations for all of us. Let me ask you this, have any of the truckers ever asked you to help divert a cargo?" The blameless interviewee acknowledges that there was some discussion but never took it seriously enough to mention. The culpable ones latch on to such discussions as an opportunity to cast blame on others and report that discussions took place.

The "Thoughts" Question   "There are so many demands and pressures on people in their daily lives, that they occasionally fantasize about doing things. Now, as far as you're concerned, do you recall ever thinking of having sex with Mary Sue even though you never actually did?" To report a fantasy of having sex with Mary Sue tells me that the culpable interviewee considers the thinking meaningful, memorable enough to recall. "Well, there have been times when she rubs herself against me and I think she really wants me to touch her sexually." The innocent do not consider such fleeting moments significant and deny involvement.

The "Borrow" Question   "It's not unusual for people to borrow from places where they work. Think back, if you will, on any time you may have borrowed money from the bank and paid it back. What comes to mind on that? Have you borrowed from the bank without permission and paid it back later?" Some delinquent people will ponder that question appearing to be weighing whether to reveal having borrowed from the bank. Others may say that they borrowed only one time, or so, but repaid it in full each time. During a bank embezzlement case I asked a young lady the "Borrow" question and she nodded her head yes, looked down, and her tears began to flow. Her answer was something like, "Well, maybe one time, but I paid it back the next day." I asked, "Do you recall how many times you borrowed and paid back?" The response was, "Only four times." I followed with, "What is the most you borrowed at any one time?" The response, "$35.00." At this point I asked, "How many times do you recall forgetting to pay back the money?" This was the beginning of an interrogation during which she admitted stealing a total of $7,000.00 from the bank. (I don't normally move into an interrogation at this time, but my intuition told me it was the thing to do then.) In this case, and in the questions that follow, a series of questions follow naturally and form a chain of testimony as the interviewee reveals more and more.

The "Instruction" Question   "Many people teach their kids about sex as they're growing up. After all, it's the responsibility of the parent to teach their children about things like health care. What comes to mind about telling your kids things about sex?" The molester may respond that he or she may have tried to teach the child how to masturbate in order to keep the child from seeking sexual pleasure elsewhere. A father may have taught his daughter how to insert a tampon. All such discussion is intended to determine if molesting actually took place, or if the interviewee has been wrongfully accused. You might say, "Now, in the process of that instruction, could you have accidentally inserted your finger between the lips of her vagina?" The blameless may say: "Not for any sexual reason." The culpable may say: "Maybe only a little and she seemed to like it."

The "Willingness" Question

"If the investigation shows that you actually did have some sexual contact with Jane, would you be willing to explain it and get this straightened out?" Without hesitation, the blameless typically say, "But, nothing happened; I didn't do anything." The culpable, after some hesitation, tend to respond, "Well, sure, but I don't recall anything like that happening."

The "Consequence" Questions

The next few questions ask the interviewee about the consequences for certain actions. For example, you might ask, "Let's assume that we find out the report was not true. What should happen to Jane for her false accusation?" or, "If we find out who did sexually touch Jane, what should happen to that person?"

The principal objective of these questions is to stimulate interviewee judgment, to encourage the interviewee to identify with or withdraw from the delinquent person. In my experience, the culpable person expresses little or no judgment against the delinquent person, while the blameless express contempt. If the interviewee does not suggest jail for the responsible party, ask, "How about jail for that person?" Innocent interviewees usually respond, "I should think so, that pervert!" or something to that effect. They answer smoothly, and give their judgment without hesitation. The deceptive, on the other hand, tend to be lenient toward the guilty party or evasive in their responses. They might say, for example, "Well, jail seems a little harsh," or "It really depends on the circumstances. Maybe the person was under a lot of strain." The molester tends to be lenient in prescribing consequences, while the blameless are often extremely harsh.

The "Kind-to-Do-It" Question   Your next question might be, "What kind of person do you think would do something like this?" Innocent people quickly provide an appropriate response like, "Some sick person!" or, "A pervert, I'd say!" The guilty will tend to rationalize or evade the question, responding, "Someone who's under a lot of pressure!" or, "I'm not that kind of person! I'm not a pervert!"

The "Why-It-Happened" Question   Then you might ask, "Why do you think the police report was made?" You might expect the deceptive to respond, "I have no idea," whereas the blameless might respond, "No reason!" or, "There's a divorce case!"

The "They-Say-You-Did-It" Question   When you ask, "Is there any reason for anyone to say you broke into the storeroom?" innocent interviewees will respond, "No, I don't think so. I didn't do it." They will appear to consider whether they could have given anyone a reason to suspect them. Rather than squirm guiltily, they may furrow their brow, squint, or look contemplative. This body language is fleeting and difficult to fake convincingly. You might ask, "Why do you think anyone would say that you stole the missing diamond ring?" The response of the blameless might be, "Well, I did handle it when it was returned to the store and I put it on my little finger for a few minutes to show it off. But I put it back in the returns drawer and I didn't see it after that. I didn't steal it." The culpable casts blame on others as in, "The whole place is not secure and I told the management that several times. Anyone could have come in here to take it."

The "They-Say-They-Saw-You" Question   Follow up the preceding question with, "Is there any reason that anyone might say they saw you breaking into the storeroom?" The innocent might say, "No, because I didn't do it!" They will respond quickly and without contemplation because they don't need "deep thought" (Yeschke, p. 92) to know what they did. The guilty party may respond hesitatingly, "Well, let me see. . . . No, I don't think so."

The "What-Would-You-Say" Question   This question asks the interviewee to think about the person responsible for the incident? Ask something like, "Let's assume the ring was actually stolen. If the guilty person were standing here before you, what would you say to him or her?" Interviewees with nothing to hide often respond, "What you did was wrong!" or, "That was a stupid thing to do!" The response will come quickly, often as an angry blast of indignation and condemnation. Deceptive interviewees will often be hard-pressed to find words of condemnation while stammering around.

The "Expanding Inquiry" Question   "Do you mind having the investigation extend beyond your family to your neighbors and coworkers?" The blameless generally won't mind having an investigator poke around his or her neighborhood, while the delinquent one may realize that if someone does go asking questions of neighbors one of the neighbors may recall seeing some indication of the stolen item in the possession of the interviewee.

Please keep in mind that none of the above questions and responses stands alone. They are used together to elicit a pattern of interviewee responses which can be used as the basis of your conclusion in the Terminal Phase.

THE TERMINAL PHASE

Between points E and F of the Polyphasic Flowchart lies the Terminal Phase, a turning point in the interview. In this phase the interviewer draws a conclusion about the interviewee's truthfulness. It is in the Terminal Phase that the investigator synthesizes all of the verbal and nonverbal responses into a significant pattern indicating either truth or deception. Such conclusions are based to some extent on how the case evidence from other sources matches up with information provided by the interviewee. If you decide the information acquired from other interviewees is credible, you will no doubt question the truthfulness of the current interviewee.

The Terminal Phase and the Follow-Up Phase combine into four steps with two steps in each phase. In the Terminal Phase, Step 1 is determining whether the interviewee has answered your questions fully and truthfully; Step 2 involves planning what to do next. By point F in the terminal phase, evaluate whether you are talking to an innocent person, whether you need to interview further to elicit concealed information, or whether you should seek a confession by moving into an interrogation.

Step 1 in the Terminal Phase

By the Terminal Phase, you will have had the opportunity to observe, evaluate, and assess the interviewee, noting how the pattern of his or her responses compares to the totality of evidence. You have gained time to become confident in your conclusion. Most interviewees are perceptive enough to realize when you have jumped to conclusions in the Primary Phase without taking the time to listen and observe accurately. Therefore, wait until the Terminal Phase to draw any conclusions about the interviewee.

Generally, one interview will offer sufficient indicators to guide your judgment, but not always. Bear in mind that a conclusion is an inference, not a fact. Assess the interviewee's candor up to the end of the Primary Phase (point E), which is essentially the last moment of non-accusatory interaction. There are certainly no absolutes in such assessments, but I'm convinced that nonverbal "signals" (Yeschke, p. 92) are meaningful indicators of deception. I think it's fair to say, based on my experience, that certain behavior signals characterize deceptive individuals while other behavior signals characterize the truthful.

Any interviewee, no matter how cooperative, might show some desire to withhold information. Witnesses may appear to withhold information when, in fact, they are self-conscious because they did not do more to catch a thief, or failed to note a license number. Victims may hide some of the details of an incident because of embarrassment at allowing someone to take advantage of them, or feeling stupid at not being able to control a stressful moment. On the other hand, inconsistencies in a victim's story usually indicate that the crime was fabricated. The witness may actually be a co-conspirator in the crime and have good reason to feel uneasy about being interviewed for further details. Just so, the thief obviously might hold back information. Thieves with little practice tend to stumble over routine investigative questions and give telltale signs of involvement.

Still, it is possible that you might reach the end of the Terminal Phase and still be uncertain about the interviewee's veracity. Better to wait than to prematurely conclude that the interviewee has been deceptive (Yeschke, p. 110). Any action you take following a rush to judgment will only increase the interviewee's reluctance to reveal the information. Rather than working with you to reveal the truth of an incident, the interviewee will focus his or her energy on self-defense. If you have to end the interview uncertain, be sure to maintain rapport with the interviewee. The Terminal Phase is not the time to use coercion or any other illegal and destructive tactics to force a resolution.

In any event, at about point E of the interview, you will probably conclude that the interviewee's verbal and nonverbal responses indicate one of the following:

- Truthfulness
- Probable truthfulness
- Possible truthfulness
- Possible deception
- Probable deception
- Deception

Now you need to decide what to do next.

Step 2 in the Terminal Phase

If this is to be the end of the interview, leave your business card and ask the interviewee to contact you if he or she remembers anything new. Maintain rapport! Alternatively, if inconsistencies remain to clarify, you might continue the interview and tell the interviewee that it looks like he or she has more information to provide. You might choose to give the impression that you suspect the interviewee of hiding significant information. If time does not allow for continuing, you might note that a second interview will be set up in the near future to review a few things. Finally, you might offer to arrange a polygraph examination to verify the honesty of the interviewee.

THE FOLLOW-UP PHASE

The last phase of the interview process is the Follow-Up Phase which occurs between points F and M on the Polyphasic Flowchart. During this final phase of the interview process, inconsistencies are resolved, confrontation may take place, and confessions may be obtained. It is time to clearly announce that you are convinced there is more information that has yet to be provided by the interviewee. "Daring" (Yeschke, p. 111) to reveal an opinion related to the interviewee's veracity may frighten the untutored investigator, but the seasoned will take the calculated risk. The investigator might announce to the victim, witness, or suspect:

- I think there's something else on your mind that you haven't told me.
- It seems to me that you're holding something back. It's important to talk to me about anything that's bothering you about this matter.
- I think you're not telling me the whole truth about this incident. I'd like to clear this matter up, and I need your help to do that.

In this phase you have considerable flexibility in applying the floating-point strategy. Maintain your rapport, continue to actively listen, and avoid radical direction or any use of abuse, coercion, harassment, or intimidation. Between flowchart points F and G you might decide to review the testimony, point out inconsistencies, and suggest deception. Then encourage truthfulness. Depending on the circumstances of the investigation, you may decide to pursue one of the following courses:

- Arrange for the interviewer to take a polygraph examination.
- Schedule a new interview with the interviewee, allowing yourself time for additional research to prepare for the interrogation.
- Begin to attempt to gain a confession from the subject.

Step 3 in the Follow-Up Phase

To verify the information provided, you might want to schedule a polygraph (detection-of-deception) examination for the interviewee. The suggestion might be made at several places during the interview process: between points F and G, between points H and I, or around point L. The timing depends on the situation and how the suggestion fits into the overall process. Some people will not agree to undergo a polygraph examination, no matter how helpful you tell them it will be. Other people will be reluctant but will eventually submit to it.

There are two important things to consider before subjecting an interviewee to a polygraph examination. First, you must be convinced that the polygraph is a practical, functional, and trustworthy investigative tool. Second, you must ensure that the forensic psychophysiologist whom you choose to administer the examination will provide high-quality professional service. Although polygraph examinations are not 100 percent accurate, they have proved to be highly reliable (Yeschke).

Step 4 in the Follow-Up Phase

After attempting to resolve inconsistencies in the interviewee's story between points F and H, you may decide to take further action. If you are convinced that the interviewee is involved, directly or indirectly, in the matter under investigation, you will reveal this between points H and I. "Interrogation might start earlier, between points F and G, but the most intense interrogating begins between points H and I" of the flowchart (Yeschke, p. 112). If you are ready to point out inconsistencies in the interviewer's story, the next thing to do is to announce your conclusion to the interviewee. To begin the interrogation, you might confront the subject by saying, for example:

- It's clear to me that you're not telling me the truth about this matter. It looks like you're involved in this.
- "Everything indicates you're the one who did it. It looks like you haven't told me the whole truth."
- "It seems to me that you are holding something back."
- "I'm uneasy about what you've told me here today. I believe you've got more to tell me."
- "I think you're the one who did it, and it's important for us to talk about this to get it cleared up."

Use care in making these comments. You do not want to frighten the subject. This is not a time for a nose-to-nose and toes-to-toes combat stance. It is a time to present yourself in a friendly way, concerned and ready to assist the subject to clarify the facts. You can turn the situation into a snarling mess or a warm hand shake. "Announcing your conclusion takes some daring and skill" (Yeschke, p. 111). Note that there is no need to accuse harshly or intimidate the interviewee. This is the time for specific review and persistent encouragement to clear up inconsistencies or gain an admission of guilt. It is at this point that the interview gradually flows into an interrogation. The interviewer-turned-interrogator now clearly and specifically announces that the subject seems to be intentionally withholding information and is probably a key player in the matter under investigation. While you do this, you must continue to help the subject save face and rationalize his or her involvement.

Up to this time, you have modified your efforts to deal with embarrassed victims and reluctant witnesses, but now is the time to proceed ahead into the interrogation to seek a confession. Don't be destructive in your efforts. Do not label the interrogatee when addressing him or her, as in, "You're the thief." Not only are such comments hostile, but they are self-defeating. If your words and actions humiliate the subject they will undoubtedly block your chances of hearing the truth.

Be certain, and be confident! This is no longer the time for the using the conditional word "if," but to display confidence in the subject's involvement. Interrogation is not for all investigators. It is a matter of temperament, confidence, and skill. Some investigators are more capable than others of handling this concentrated search for the truth. If you judgmentally denounce the interrogatee when you reach your opinion, you cannot expect to gain a legally acceptable admission of guilt.

Your efforts may yield only an incomplete admission of guilt. If you doubt that the subject told the complete story of what happened, remember that even a partial confession—as long as it was legally obtained—can be helpful in resolving the investigation. This is not to say that you should be satisfied with a half-done job. Accept whatever confession is offered, have it witnessed and put into written form. Then commit yourself to starting over with renewed effort to seek additional details of the subject's culpability.

REVIEW QUESTIONS

Answer the following questions and explain your answers fully.

Primary Phase

1. What is the purpose of the Primary Phase?

2. What are semi-structured questions?

Bones (skeletal constructs)

1. What is non-accusatory questioning?

2. Will using compassion help the interviewer?

3. What is the principal objective of semi-structured questions in the primary phase?

4. What is the significance of having the interviewee provide a narrative of an incident?

5. How is the conditional word "if" be used in the interview process?

6. What verbal indicators of deception show up in the use of semi-structured questions?

7. What nonverbal indicators of deception show up in the use of semi-structured questions?

8. Does it matter if the interviewee identifies with the culpable one?

9. In the Primary Phase, when do you come to a conclusion about interviewee deception?

The Terminal Phase

1. What is the purpose of the Terminal Phase?

2. What range of conclusions might the interviewer make about the interviewee's veracity?

3. Are there absolute behavior signals characteristic of deception?

The Follow-Up Phase

1. If you confront the subject as a beginning of an interrogation, is it okay to be abusive?

2. Is there any value in the continued use of filter factors?

3. What might you say to the subject as you begin an interrogation?

4. Does it take some daring to reveal your opinion without using coercion or intimidation?

5. Can a polygraph examination be of investigative use?

6. When is it a good time to condemn the interrogatee?

REFERENCES

Yeschke, Charles L. *Interviewing: A Forensic Guide to Interrogation*, 2nd ed. Springfield, IL: Charles C Thomas, 1993.

9

Setting, Location, Intensity, and Approach in the Interview

To help ensure the success of an interview, the investigator must take into consideration many factors, including where the interview will take place, where the participants will be located within the interview room, how intensely the interviewer will press for information, and what approach he or she will use in questioning the interviewee. All of these elements require careful planning because they have a significant impact on the outcome of every interview. This chapter suggests ways in which environmental setting, participant location, intensity, and approach can be incorporated into the interview process.

ENVIRONMENTAL SETTING

Privacy is a key element of successful interviews. When possible, arrange to conduct your interviews in a comfortable, private room away from the busy flow of people. The environment you choose should be quiet and free from disturbances. Don't inconvenience the interviewee by insisting on a distant site for the interview, however. There is little to gain by transporting the interviewee some distance to a site you believe to be ideal. It stands to reason that the place for interviewing, if in your total control, should be neat, clean, and generally comfortable with regard to heating, air conditioning, lighting, and so forth. But, obviously, less than perfect conditions are not going to stop you from interviewing someone if you're at the end of the bar in a dimly lit tavern or in an apartment hallway hazy with the remains of smoke from burned garbage. The key factor in any interview is privacy, and most sites that provide privacy are probably suitable.

LOCATION OF PARTICIPANTS

Location of interview participants is more than the distances between them during the interview. It includes the question of anything being between them, such as a desk, and where the exit is located in relation to the participants.

Personal Space

There is an invisible boundary, known as personal space, around each of us. We become uncomfortable when strangers intrude in our personal space. Most Americans reserve about a foot and a half of space around them for intimate conversation. They allow casual interactions in the space between a foot and a half to about four feet. Impersonal transactions take place beyond about four feet. Personal space varies not only with culture (Hall), but also with social status. People of high status assume and are granted more personal space than people of lower status. With over one hundred sixty countries in the world, it is reasonable to consider each culture to have its own customs. How we smell, our odor, what we wear, where we stand and sit when we converse, and other factors make up the differences between cultures. The main consideration in dealing with a variety of cultures is that we be sensitive to them all even though we don't know the particulars of each. Living in a melting pot of cultures called the United States of America requires us to respect and adapt to each culture so that we don't insult anyone unnecessarily.

Proxemics is the study of the spatial distances that people maintain between themselves and others. A knowledge of proxemics can help you become a better interviewer. Whether standing or seated during an interview, be sensitive to the interviewee's level of comfort, and use it to determine how the interviewee defines his or her personal space. Enter this space with care to avoid alarming the interviewee.

As you begin the interview, position yourself about six feet away from the interviewee so you won't frighten or anger the interviewee. I find that beginning interview interactions with about six feet between participants doesn't seem to offend anyone, be they male, female, young, old, victim, witness, suspect, or from various cultural backgrounds. It is from the distance of six feet and closer that warrants care and consideration, because to move too close too fast may cause the interviewee discomfort and interrupt rapport. As the interview progresses, move your chair closer. Not only does this convey your warmth, but it will help you and the interviewee focus more fully on the discussion.

Conversation, Moderate, and Intimate Locations

It is my experience that three distinct distances can be identified between participants in an interview. In order of decreasing physical distance, I call these the conversation, moderate, and intimate locations (Yeschke). When I mention location I include distance and position. Most interviews take place in the conversation or moderate locations.

The Conversation Location   In the conversation location, the interview participants are located about six feet apart, as shown in Figures 9-1 and 9-2. This is a "safe" distance for the interviewee, just beyond easy physical reach. In this location, participants have enough room to lean forward without touching and can move their legs comfortably. In the conversation location, the interviewer can watch the interviewee for nonverbal communication at critical moments. That is, it is obviously easier to see the interviewee wiggle a foot while in the conversation location, which may be significant to the investigator's overall efforts at observation and evaluation. The conversation location is used between points A and C on the Polyphasic Flowchart shown in Figure 7-1 in Chapter 7.

At the beginning of the interview, position your chair to the left or right of the interviewee's chair at an angle of about 45 degrees. Avoid facing the interviewee squarely and symbolically presenting yourself as a threat. There should be no obstruction between you and the interviewee other than possibly the corner of a desk. In this setting, you may lean back or forward in your chair, depending on the context of the interview. However, avoid leaning your chair back against a wall, and don't put your feet up on the desk. Keep your body position alert, projecting an attentive professional manner at all times. Begin the interview with yourself and the interviewee in the conversation location, about six feet apart. Be careful not to violate the interviewee's personal

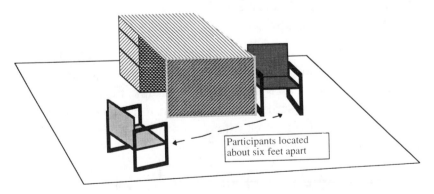

Participants located
about six feet apart

Figure 9-1. Conversation Location

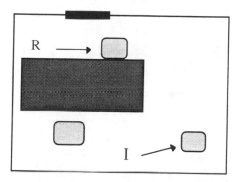

Figure 9-2. Conversation Location: Plan View of Typical Interview Room, 10 by 12 feet. I = Interviewer; R = Respondent

space. If you go past that invisible line and step into the interviewee's "flight area," he or she will generally back off to increase the space between you. The interviewee's flight area is located somewhere in the moderate location.

Moderate Location   The moderate location brings the interview participants to within about four feet of one another. This is close enough to allow the interviewer to gently touch the interviewee's arm or shoulder if appropriate. The moderate location is illustrated in Figures 9-3 and 9-4. Figure 9-5 illustrates the times

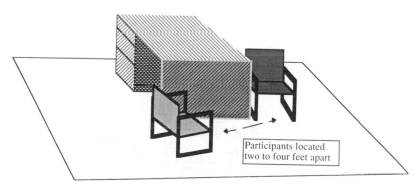

Participants located two to four feet apart

Figure 9-3. Moderate Location

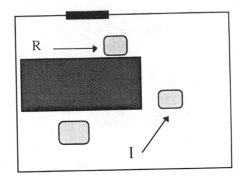

Figure 9-4.   Moderate Location: Plan View of Typical Interview Room, 10 by 12 feet. I = Interviewer; R = Respondent

during which location changes and intensity levels may shift during the interview process. (Intensity levels are covered later in this chapter.) Depending on the strategy used, the process is intended to smoothly slide from the interview into the interrogation as appropriate.

In the moderate location, the participants are generally situated at a 45-degree angle, as in the conversation location. At this distance, legs must be crossed carefully. Most interviews and many interrogations can be conducted from the moderate location. Avoid rushing from the conversation location into the moderate location. Moving closer to the interviewee too soon may seem like crowding the interviewee and cause undue stress. Although stress is built into every interview, creating undue stress

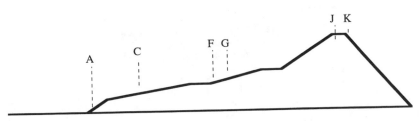

Figure 9-5.   Strategy Points and Intensity Level Shifts in the Interview Process

may block the flow of communication; this is unnecessary and self-defeating.

The Intimate Locations   In the intimate location, the participants are at first situated about two feet apart, as illustrated in Figures 9-6 and 9-7. As the intensity of the interview increases, the interviewer moves to within about a foot of the interviewee and shifts position somewhat, as shown in Figures 9-8 and 9-9. Points F and I in Figure 9-10 depict times during the interview process when your strategy and location may shift. Resolving inconsistencies generally begins at point F of the flowchart. Interrogations generally begin at point I. The gradual increase in height represented on the flowchart in Figure 9-5 from point A to F, then to I, then to J, represent the increases in the intensity level of review and encouragement.

The investigator's shift in position from intimate location 1 to intimate location 2 often accompanies a change in the interview strategy from resolving inconsistencies (interviewing) to gaining an admission of guilt (interrogating). The investigator should make this transition smoothly, not only in shifting position but also in the comments, questions, and intensity he or she employs.

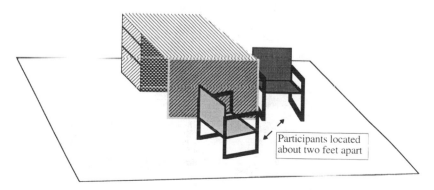

Participants located about two feet apart

Figure 9-6.   Intimate Location 1

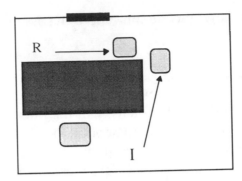

Figure 9-7. Intimate Location 1: Plan View of Typical Interview
Room, 10 by 12 feet. I = Interviewer; R = Respondent

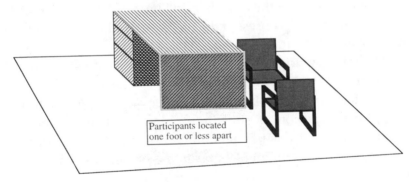

Figure 9-8. Intimate Location 2

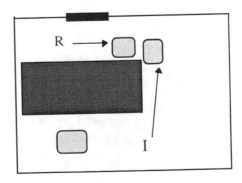

Figure 9-9. Intimate Location 2: Plan View of Typical Interview
Room, 10 by 12 feet. I = Interviewer; R = Respondent

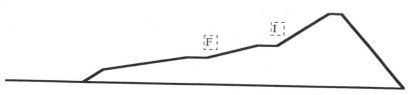

Figure 9-10.   Intensity Level Elevation: Illustrates Intensity Level Shift from Points F and I

In the intimate locations, the rhetorical questions and statements used are different from the interviewer's previous efforts. In these locations, interviewing may no longer be the objective. Interrogation may be at work where admissions and confession are sought. The intimate location may be the most stressful or the most reassuring, depending on how the interview is conducted. In this location, you can easily reach the interviewee. Your chair is situated quite close to the interviewee's chair, so that your knee is next to the interviewee's knee. In this location, the crossing of legs is next to impossible. This distance is reserved for in-depth interviews requiring intense interpersonal communication, great empathy, and lots of encouragement. It is also used for interrogations in which a confession or admission is sought.

It is not always possible or necessary to employ all three locations in one interview. The setup of the interview room sometimes prevents the interviewer from moving closer to the interviewee than the moderate location (about four feet), and space limitations sometimes make it impossible to begin an interview in the conversation location. The intimate locations are generally not used unless the investigator is dealing with an interviewee who needs consoling or the investigator has made the shift from interview to interrogation.

REVIEW AND ENCOURAGEMENT INTENSITIES

Throughout the interview, the investigator reviews the facts of the case and their related implications with the interviewee and encourages him or her to answer questions truthfully. The intensity of this review and encouragement varies through the different phases of the interview process. Throughout this section please refer to Figure 9-11, which shows a schematic for the various terms we will be using. We will be using letter symbols to represent the different kinds and degrees of review and encouragement. First we will discuss and define review, encouragement, and intensity.

In general, review (R) and encouragement (E) are your two main tools in the interview. You can use them with a light touch or with firm control. You will use R and E in different ways and at different times during the interview process. It is the degree to which you use them that makes the difference. I call this "degree intensity," to indicate the degree of effort and concentration with which you use the tools of review and encouragement.

Certainly, by the energy of your words and actions, by the unwavering concentration on the issue, the interviewer's intensity influences the respondent. Show your earnestness to get to the truth by a zeal and a human warmth that will not give up. Your evident dedication to the objective draws the interviewee into your concentrated effort. Used properly throughout the interview, the effects of R and E range from reassurance, to revealing deception, to inviting an admission of guilt. Used improperly, R and E cause defensiveness and rebellion.

The negative use of R (review) might be something like: "Each time I interview someone in this case, your name comes up

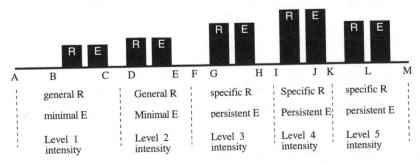

Figure 9-11. Intensity Levels of Review and Encouragement

as the one that stole the money! What do you have to say for yourself?" The negative use of E (encouragement) might be: "I know you did this theft, you low life! When are you going to wise up and stop being stupid and show that you have some smarts after all?"

Review   The topics you choose to review with the interviewee vary with the phases of the interview and the facets of the investigation. Too, each investigative topic may require differing amounts of review as you move through the interview process. From the Initial Phase through Follow-Up and moving from the general to the gradually more specific, the investigator's level of review might increase as follows:

- Inquiry into the circumstances of the matter under investigation.
- Discussion regarding the interviewee's knowledge, opportunity, access, and motivation pertaining to the matter under investigation.
- Coverage of the totality of the circumstances as related to the interviewee's knowledge, opportunity, access, and motivation.
- Considering the totality of the circumstances in lesser or greater depth.
- Considering the interviewee's relationship to the totality of the circumstances with less or more focus.

Encouragement   The reason to encourage the interviewee is to reassure and reach a certain objective—the truth. During the process of trying to reach that goal, only positive methods to encourage the interviewee to tell the truth are suggested:

- Persuading
- Selling
- Influencing
- Calling for the truth

Intensity Levels

Below we will look at each intensity level and illustrate the specific kinds of review (R) and encouragement (E) that operate at each level.

Level 1: *general Review and minimal Encouragement*
(gRmE)   Level 1 is generally used in all interviews from point A to between points C and D on the Polyphasic Flowchart. In Level 1, the least amount of effort is employed in using review and encouragement. No attempt is made to point out gaps or inconsistencies in the interviewee's story. Level 1 is also used for the preliminary inquiry during the precontact section of the initial phase. While learning the details regarding the matter under investigation, it isn't appropriate to challenge the information. If it becomes necessary, there will be a time for that later.

Level 2: *General Review and Minimal Encouragement*
(GRME)   This level, used from between points C and D to point F on the flowchart, represents the greatest amount of general review and minimal encouragement. Compared to Level 1, there is more effort in this level to use review and encouragement. No gaps in the interviewee's story are pointed out or challenged, but some effort is made to clarify details. During this level, the semi-structured questions discussed in Chapter 8 are used to draw out the truth. At this level, interviewees may, through verbal or nonverbal signs, indicate that they are attempting to dodge your questions or provide dishonest answers.

Level 3: *specific Review and persistent Encouragement*
(sRpE)   Used between points F and I of the flowchart, this level involves the least amount of specific review and persistent encouragement. In this level, the interviewer discusses any inconsistencies that he or she has noticed in the interviewee's responses. This is not the time to interrogate, but rather the time to revisit investigative detail. The interviewer must be bold

enough to state clearly that there are inconsistencies that must be resolved. He or she must persuade (E) the interviewee that it is inevitable that the truth will eventually be discovered. During this level, culpable individuals will probably reveal further signs of their deception. Then it is time for the interviewer to take on the role of interrogator and look for an admission or confession. The interviewer puts on a different hat, so to speak, becoming assertive and more determined. Between H and I of the process, the interrogator begins to sell (E) the subject on the idea of telling the truth "to get this thing cleared up." Having taken this road, the interrogator should not back down easily—only if he or she becomes convinced it is the wrong direction.

Don't rush to use intensity Level 3 with interviewees as soon as you notice inconsistencies. Make it a general rule to tune in to inconsistencies during the Primary Phase. Throughout the interview, gradually focus more attention on the inconsistencies and become more assertive in pointing out gaps in the interviewee's story. Become less accepting of excuses as you begin to challenge the patterns of deception. Sell (E) the interviewee on the idea of willingly divulging the truth.

Level 4: Specific Review and Persistent Encouragement (SRPE)
This level, used between points I and K on the flowchart, represents a greater intensity of specific review and persistent encouragement than Level 3. Most interviewees never reach this level of interaction because the investigator decides they are being truthful. Remember, it is a mistake to interrogate all interviewees as though they were guilty or lying. Level 4 reaches its greatest intensity between points J and K as the interrogator attempts to gain a confession or admission. (A confession includes several significant culpable statements or all such statements, whereas an admission deals with one or more culpable statement.) Sometimes even the "victim" is considered to be deceptive and then interrogated. This level of intensity includes greater efforts to assist the subject to rationalize and save face while he or

she confesses total or partial responsibility for the matter under investigation.

Level 5: specific Review persistent Encouragement (sRpE)

Level 5 is used between points K and M on the flowchart. It represents about the same intensity of specific review and persistent encouragement as Level 3. During this level, the interrogatee may have provided an admission but not a complete confession. At point L, the investigator must decide whether to ask the subject to undergo a polygraph examination to confirm the professed limited nature of his or her involvement.

APPROACHES

The interview process outlined in this book involves three approaches built around the kinds of questions asked. They are the Structured Approach, the Semi-Structured Approach, and the Non-Structured Approach. In a structured approach, the questions address topics such as the spelling of the interviewee's last name, date of birth, number of years of education; in essence, they are fact-finding questions. Semi-structured questions form a matrix around the incident under investigation. They allow more room for discussion as the interviewer probes for opinions, perceptions, and direct information about the incident. Most especially, through semi-structured questions the interviewer probes for responses or behavior that reveals truthfulness or deception. The non-structured approach is the most flexible of the three. Non-structured questions allow the investigator greater imagination and flexibility to resolve inconsistencies in the interviewee's responses, and, occasionally, move toward an interrogation and admission of guilt.

These approaches directly influence question formulation in the degree of intensity, and the coverage from general to specific in review and encouragement. While the structured questions used in the Initial Phase have no specific relation to the investigation, the semi-structured and non-structured do have a specific relationship.

The Structured Approach

The structured approach is used at the beginning of the interview and forms the basis of the investigator's direct observation, evaluation, and assessment of the interviewee. This approach begins at point A on the Polyphasic Flowchart and ends between points C and D. The questions asked during the structured portion of the interview require less thought from the interviewee than those asked during the semi-structured and non-structured modes. In this portion of the interview, the investigator uses basic fact-finding questions without accusation or intimidation. The investigator encourages the interviewee to comply by asking questions that he or she can answer easily. I use routine questions for this purpose, related to such things as the spelling of the interviewee's name, number of years of schooling, type of work done in the past, and so forth. These are topics to which the interviewee can easily respond. I do not ask for factual information regarding the matter under investigation during the "first four minutes or so of the interview" (Yeschke, p. 91). During the structured portion of the interview, the investigator is given the opportunity to note the interviewee's interaction status. That is, whether or not the interviewee is taking on a bold assertive role, a cooperative role, or a submissive role. Being bold, confident, and without defensiveness tends to signify truthfulness.

At first, you can expect some delay in the interviewee's response. This should not automatically be considered a significant indication of potential deception. Note how clearly the interviewee answers questions; this will help you determine the interviewee's ability to handle more complex questions later in the interview. Similarly, during the structured portion of the interview, the interviewee has the opportunity to evaluate the investigator and determine whether he or she will be treated fairly.

Everything the investigator does sends a signal to the interviewee. Every part of the investigator's presentation encourages or discourages the interviewee to comply. Of course, if the interviewee is hostile by nature to everyone in authority or is determined to lie, little of what you say or do during the interview will make much difference. Often, however, you can nudge reluctant interviewees into a more compliant stance and may even eventually encourage deceptive interviewees to provide an admission or confession. The structured portion of the interview is the time to begin building rapport with the interviewee. The structured approach can help establish the relative status of the interview participants, and it assists in creating a secure feeling for both.

Toward the end of the structured approach there is a transition into the Primary Phase: the gRmE level sounds something like: "Nancy, as I've mentioned, the reason I'm talking to various employees is to try to find out what happened to the missing money (gR). I'd like to get it back if possible and I'd like to make some recommendations to the company about how to prevent this from happening in the future. I need you to work with me on this to clear up this matter (mE). If you will share with me anything that comes to mind as we go along it would be helpful (mE)."

As the investigator enters the Primary Phase, the GRME sounds something like this: "Nancy, as I've said, I don't know if the money is stolen or if something else caused the loss. I understand that the money was on the counter when the fight took place in the parking lot (GR). Now, if you took that money it's important to tell me about that (ME). How do you stand on that; did you steal that money? (ME). Okay then, you had nothing to do with that loss then? Let me ask. Do you know who did actually steal that money?"

The Semi-Structured Approach

The semi-structured approach begins at about point C of the flowchart. Using this approach implies your desire to receive information from the interviewee in an immediate way; however, it does not imply the use of coercion, abuse, or intimidation. When I say in an immediate way, I mean without delay and kept to the point, befitting the question. If the interviewee nervously starts to ramble with comments outside of the confines of the question, I try to gently nudge the responses back to the topic. I try to stay on track by following my planned interview, all the while making a mental note of the interviewee's possible efforts to sidetrack my progress. Accusation and confrontation are not appropriate at this time.

With the semi-structured approach, you must be tuned in to what is happening moment by moment. You must be alert for signs that the truth is trying to show itself. Look for signals and patterns of deception. "The formulation of questions in the semi-structured portion of the interview is not materially altered by the interviewee's responses" (Yeschke, p. 92). The questions are partly intended to stimulate the interviewee to exhibit verbal or nonverbal signals indicative of deception. In formulating your questions, follow the samples described in Chapter 8. Continue to formulate your questions as suggested until you are confident that the interviewee's responses signal deception.

The Non-Structured Approach

At about points F and G of the interview interaction, you may decide to alter your interview strategy and use specific review and persistent encouragement (sRpE) to resolve inconsistencies in the interviewee's story. The interviewee's reluctance to provide truthful information or outright hostility might be the basis for a greater intensity of review and encouragement. Between points F and G, you might decide to follow up on patterns in the interviewee's responses that you believe signal deception. This turning point requires delicate handling. If you act prematurely, your change in strategy might spark greater reluctance on the part of the interviewee. Between points F and H, after attempting to resolve inconsistencies, you may decide to proclaim clearly your belief in the interviewee's culpability and begin an interrogation.

Proficient interrogators move smoothly and cleverly to help the interrogatee reveal the truth.

PUTTING IT ALL TOGETHER

As shown in Figure 9-12, there is a clear relationship between the levels of intensity and the three approaches used during the interview process. During the first part of the interview, the investigator uses the structured approach and Level 1 intensity simultaneously. As he or she begins to use the semi-structured approach, the intensity increases to Level 2. Finally, as the investigator attempts to resolve inconsistencies in the interviewee's story, he or she employs the non-structured approach and intensity levels 3, 4, and 5.

With the participants in the Conversation Location, the approach ranges from structured to semi-structured. Touching does not occur. The intensity of review and encouragement stays in the general and minimal ranges varying from gRme to GRME.

In the Moderate Location, the following intensity levels of review and encouragement are used: gRmE, GRME, and sRpE. When using gRmE and GRME intensities, the distance between participants is about four feet. While using sRpE, the participant distance varies from four feet to two feet. Reassuring touch is not used while applying gRmE or GRME, but it can be used when employing sRpE at a distance of about two feet. Between points G and K, the distance between participants varies when using

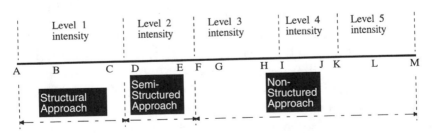

Figure 9-12. Levels of Intensity and Approaches

sRpE and SRPE intensities. The distance between the participants in the moderate location varies with the intensity of the interaction. From points C to G on the flowchart, the participants maintain a distance of about four feet; from G to J, two to four feet; from J to K, about two feet. In the moderate location, the semi-structured and non-structured approaches of question formulation can be used. Between points F and G, the interviewer might announce that there appear to be inconsistencies in the information that the interviewee has provided.

The Intimate Location is used with the Level 4 intensity of review and encouragement, from SRPE to sRpE. Intimate implies a closeness, a warmth which may strengthen rapport and stimulate greater cooperation. Confrontations about inconsistencies take place in this location, as well as the beginnings of interrogation.

REVIEW QUESTIONS

Answer the following questions and explain your answers fully.

Overview, Environment, and Location

1. What are some factors to consider in making the interview a success?

2. Is privacy a key element to successful interviewing?

3. What may happen if you invade the personal space of an interviewee?

4. What is proxemics?

5. How are the three locations used in the interview process?

6. Will using the conversation location offend anyone?

7. What is the flight area?

8. Is the moderate location only used with interviewing rather than interrogation?

9. Is the intimate location only used for interrogation?

10. Is there a difference between interviewing and interrogating as far as your objective is concerned?

Review and Encouragement Intensities

1. How can review and encouragement be applied to strategically reach the truth?

2. Does applying review and encouragement require some subtle skills?

3. How can you use your words and actions to bring your message alive during the interview?

4. What is the objective of using varying levels of review and encouragement?

5. Is it appropriate to confront the interviewee using Level 2 intensity?

6. When are inconsistencies challenged?

7. Is it okay to interrogate each interviewee as though culpable?

8. What is the investigator trying to do by using the structured approach?

9. How can you build rapport using the structured approach?

10. What is meant by a turning point in strategy as related to points F and G of the flowchart?

REFERENCES

Hall, E.T. *The Hidden Dimension*. New York: Doubleday, 1966.

Yeschke, Charles L. *Interviewing: A Forensic Guide to Interrogation*. 2nd ed. Springfield, IL: Charles C Thomas, 1993.

10

Questions and Questioning

Interviewing is a process used to gather testimonial evidence; it has a predetermined objective—the discovery of the truth about the matter under investigation. That process defines the "playing field, players, and boundaries," and involves the asking and answering of questions. Questions vary depending on when they are asked during the interview. Because the same basic questions are used with each interviewee regardless of what is being investigated, the investigator waits until he or she reaches the point of the nonstructured approach, when specific review and persistent encouragement can resolve inconsistencies and introduce interrogation. As you ask a question in the nonstructured approach, you are listening for a response that will give you some hint about how to formulate the next question.

QUESTION FORMULATION

A question is a direct or implied request for the interviewee to think about a particular matter. Comments based on assumptions can be regarded as questions if they invite the interviewee to answer. Interview questions are the keys to an interviewee's knowledge and feelings. Keep them simple to encourage the interviewee to answer. Regard the interview as a conversation, not a cross-examination. "Do not grill the interviewee as a prosecuting attorney might do. Ask questions in a conversational manner, because your purpose is to hold a conversation with someone who has knowledge or has experienced something that you want to know about. Holding a conversation implies a certain amount of give-and-take during the interview. Make sure that you are asking questions and not making statements that do not call for answers" (Downs et al.).

Phrasing and Presenting Questions

Trust yourself to ask properly worded questions spontaneously with a natural manner. Make your questions specific, definite, and concrete. Vague, general questions allow the interviewee to evade the truth. Make your questions more pointed and complex after evaluating the degree of the interviewee's compliance. Direct the interview unobtrusively. Often, once interviewees decide to provide information, you only need to guide the flow of information with timely encouragement. Decide when to listen, when to talk, and when to observe. With overly talkative interviewees or those who wander from the point, gently lead them back, using leading questions to redirect them to the immediate issue.

The assumptions implied in your questions and the phrases you use in asking them may arouse different reactions in interviewees—cooperation, apathy, suspicion, and hostility. Some interviewees will be extremely cooperative and try to answer all questions even if the questions are poorly phrased or reveal an interviewer's false assumptions or biases. Other interviewees will be less cooperative. Keep in mind that your vocabulary could cause embarrassment or resentment. When interviewees do not understand the words you use, they may become embarrassed or insulted, refuse to cooperate, or just lie. Interviewees generally welcome the opportunity to answer questions when they can, and they feel more free to talk about familiar topics. Try to avoid using legal-sounding words like homicide, rape, and assault in your questioning because they can cause defensiveness. Interviewees who have become embarrassed or upset over a question will avoid eye contact and may display signs of discomfort or distress. Some interviewees appear shifty-eyed when they are lying, planning to lie, or are asked to reveal personal information about themselves (see Chapter 1 on self-disclosure and deception).

Asking questions accusingly or suspiciously may arouse tension—not cooperation. Abruptly asked or tricky questions are not appropriate, and are mostly self-defeating. Be sure not to ask questions in a belligerent or sarcastic manner. The nature of the interview with its question-answer pattern places you in the position of authority. Your questioning may suggest that only you know what is important and relevant. Questions that begin, "Isn't it true that you . . ." tend to be abrasive and promote defensiveness. Therefore, present your questions objectively. Avoid giving the impression that you have taken sides in the investigation. Maintain a neutral stance or the interviewee may suspect that you intend ridicule. Once you have earned dislike and resistance, you may never establish the rapport necessary to unraveling the truth. It is self-defeating to box interviewees into a corner.

To emphasize your genuine interest in the information the interviewee has provided and to strengthen the interviewee's positive view of your thoroughness, review any details during questioning. This will allow coverage of more specific areas of interest as the need arises. Make it appear that some details are not as clear as they could be, or claim to have missed some meaningful segments. Some interviewees elaborate more freely when they are asked fewer questions and are permitted to ramble a bit, so rather than ask a long series of questions, be brief and allow the interviewee to free-associate. Ideally, information-gathering interviews should reveal facts rather than opinions or feelings. Novice interviewers generally collect more opinions and feelings than facts (Banaka), so be ready to distinguish factual data from emotional comments, and to separate interviewees' observations from their interpretations.

Principles of Question Formulation

The following guidelines and those in Chapter 8 will help you formulate effective interview questions:

- Avoid third-degree questioning.
- Use closed questions when appropriate (see Chapter 7 for structured questions).
- Use open questions when appropriate (see Chapter 8 for semi-structured and nonstructured questions).
- Keep your questions simple.
- Avoid asking questions with more than one meaning.
- Dare to ask tough questions.
- Assume a positive response.
- Use leading questions when attempting to assist the interviewee to rationalize or save face.
- Ask self-appraisal questions. For example: "Has there been any time when you have thought of stealing from the company, even though you never actually did?"
- Handle trial-balloon questions cautiously.
- Assume that more information is available.

TYPES OF QUESTIONS

Knowing how to use various questions is like knowing how to use special codes that unlock a storehouse of information, in this case, the memory of the interviewee. This section explores the types of questions that can reveal your interest in the interviewee and the matter under investigation, express empathy, and promote human interaction. With a broader look at the types of questions you will become better equipped to discover information.

Two main types of questions are generally asked during investigative interviews:

1. Closed questions usually require a simple yes or no answer, or the undeniable fact such as name, address, and so on. Use this type at the beginning of interviews (see Chapter 7, "The Initial Phase") to encourage affirmative responses and to put interviewees more at ease. Later in the interview closed questions hamper your effort to discover information.

2. Open questions begin with a stated or implied who, where, what, when, how, and why and cannot be answered yes or no. They require the interviewee to think clearly, and although they can trigger the most distress in the interviewee, they also reveal the greatest amount of information.

Closed Questions

Closed questions require only a simple answer. Examples include yes-or-no questions and multiple-choice questions. They are useful when you want to maintain maximum control over the interview and save time because they limit the interviewee's response options. They are also used with reluctant interviewees who are not expected to give detailed explanations. Closed questions have the advantage of eliciting details, but they can inhibit the development of rapport. They are misused if the interviewer uses closed questions for detailed probing before the interviewee is ready. People will be willing to provide details, particularly about sensitive subjects, only if they feel comfortable.

Open Questions

Open questions help interviews flow by tapping an interviewee's objective and subjective thinking. The investigator may ask the sample questions, "Why would anyone think you had something to do with the loss? Is there something that you have said or done that would have provoked suspicion?" With these questions, you are asking the interviewee to reflect on real events and their appearances. The innocent may say, "Well, I did pay off several bills just after the loss, but I got that money from my uncle." The guilty may say: "Well, I, ah, no, not that I can think of." This interviewee, however, took an expensive vacation and bought a new car soon after the theft. Why didn't the interviewee mention the car and vacation?

A question beginning with "Why" is a particularly tricky question because it can sound challenging. It asks the interviewee to think, and, furthermore, to reveal those private thoughts. Revelation leaves the interviewee open to judgment. You need to learn the cause, reason, or purpose, but the interviewee's answer may leave him or her open to rejection and misunderstanding. An interviewee may withdraw into silence or prevaricate. Anticipate the impact of each question you use, and be careful in formulating them. Open questions can help you:

- Discover the interviewee's priorities, attitudes, needs, values, and aspirations.
- Determine the interviewee's frame of reference, and assist in establishing empathic understanding.
- Build and enhance rapport.
- Engage in active listening, stroking, and positive regard.
- Allow and encourage the interviewee to express feelings and facts without feeling threatened.
- Promote catharsis or expression of the interviewee's emotions.

There are a variety of types of open questions, each with its own characteristics and use. Reflective, directive, pointed, indirect, self-appraisal, diversion, and leading questions are discussed below. Kept sharp and ready through practice, these questions do more than probe—they set the stage for subsequent questions.

Reflective Questions   Reflective questions act like mirrors reflecting the interviewee's comments. They are used to handle objections from the interviewee, and often take the form of, "Let me see if I've got this straight . . ." or, "What I hear you say, then, is that you prefer not to comment about what you know because you don't want what you say get back to Bob, is that right? Well, let me assure you that what we talk about is confidential and I won't tell Bob about our talk." Having said this, repeat the question that triggered the interviewee's objection. By removing the obstacle to cooperation, you assist the interviewee to feel more comfortable responding to your subsequent questions.

Directive Questions   Directive questions are used to direct the interviewee's attention to areas of common ground with the investigator. Interviewees often need to hear the advantages of cooperation. They are in unknown territory with unknowable consequences, and a directive question answers this concern, as in: "You do want to get to the bottom of this, don't you? I would think you'd want your side of the story in the report so that no one misunderstands what happened," or, "I'm sure you don't want anyone to think you tried to hurt her, isn't that so?"

Pointed Questions   Pointed questions stir interviewees into action. They are specific in nature and design, pointing most precisely at the goal. Pointed questions are complex, detailed, and persuasive. Most of the questions asked in forensic interviews are pointed questions. By asking exactly what is desired, these questions show interviewees that you believe they are ready, willing, and able to respond. These questions, which are based on the self-fulfilling prophecy, work most of the time. Pointed questions need not be offensive or accusatory. On the contrary, they must be thoughtfully developed and subtly applied to avoid provoking stress and defensiveness in the interviewee. You can gently stimulate the interviewee's thinking with pointed, creative questions. For example, if you believe that the interviewee accidentally set a fire, you might ask, "On the day of the fire, how often did you smoke in the storeroom?"

Indirect Questions   Pointed questions are not always appropriate. Indirect questions are sometimes more successful because they help interviewees save face and rationalize their behavior. Indirect questions allow the interviewee to express his or her opinions, suggestions, feelings, and so on. They give the interviewee a sense of permission by taking the form, "I've talked to many of the other employees, and they believe that . . . Do you agree?" Indirect questions help you understand the interviewee's thoughts, needs, and values. Questions of this type are often used at the beginning of an interview and as a change of pace during the course of the discussion. They can also be used as diversion questions (see below).

Self-Appraisal Questions   Self-appraisal questions are used to stimulate conversation, encourage the interviewee to identify with the delinquent, and reveal truthfulness or deception. These questions might take the form: "If you are faced with a lot of pressures at home and you had all this temptation here at work with all of this money, what would prevent you from stealing?" or "Have you ever thought of stealing any money here, even though you never did?" or, "Is it possible you may have been seen in the area of the money, even for a brief time?" Self-appraisal questions help the investigator develop an hypothesis about who, how, and why an incident took place. When asking such questions, the investigator uses a floating-point strategy (see Chapter 7) to find solid ground upon which to build a hypothesis. This hypothesis is confirmed or modified by interviewee responses which may reveal information, distress, or evasion.

That which is deeply rooted in your being determines your verbal and nonverbal responses. If I asked you if you think abortion is good or bad, your response will reflect your deeply rooted conviction. The circumstances, however, will influence the candor of your response. If you know that I am a strong advocate of abortion, but I am your friend or colleague, or even more powerfully, your supervisor, you will probably modify your comments to prevent revealing the strength of your position. This modification is extremely difficult to hide. To modify responses to self-appraisal questions, the interviewee first has to think of an answer, decide that the answer would not sound good, then make up a new story, and tell it convincingly. It is almost impossible for deceptive or evasive interviewees to be consistent in answering self-appraisal questions.

Diversion Questions   Diversion questions have two purposes: they distract the interviewee's thoughts from a tension-producing issue, and they build rapport between the investigator and the interviewer. To temporarily divert an interviewee's anger or fear may be extremely difficult because the strength of that anger or fear is so strong that clear thinking is all but eliminated. Diversion questions are useful when dealing with highly emotional interviewees. Their use delays the inquiry into the specific nature of the incident until the interviewee has regained his or her composure.

As an illustration, when talking with a customer that witnessed a bank robbery, it was evident that she was shaken by her experience. She needed time to realize that the danger was over. Therefore, I spoke with firm reassurance that all was safe. I tried to break her focus on the fear caused by the robbery and help her think clearly about what she saw. Initially in a state of shock, her thinking hazy, she gradually began to sense that she could relax. My diversion questions dealt with topics unrelated to the robbery, questions she could answer with ease such as, "What type of work do you do Mary?" and, "Have you lived in this community many years?" Gradually she became able to focus her thoughts on what she saw and heard during the robbery.

Diversion questions often focus on someone or something more important and attractive to the interviewee than the incident under investigation. I was called in by a business owner to investigate a burglary which had been reported to the local police. The incident involved the theft of about $3,000 from a retail business. The money had been stored in a file cabinet. The details of the crime are not, now, as critical as the police response and the owner's angry reaction to that response. The first, and only, police officer at the crime scene told the owner that, in all probability, no fingerprints had been left at the crime scene. No detective arrived to search for evidence or conduct interviews. The case was administratively closed, all of which infuriated the owner.

The main point here is that the owner, in the process of providing me with preliminary information, was preoccupied with the "bad job" done by the police rather than the details that might help me fulfill my obligations. To refocus the owner's anger, I diverted attention from the crime in an attempt to quell that anger and disappointment. I said something like, "You certainly have a beautiful place here, it looks like your people take pride in their work!" He responded, and I said: "It must have taken many years to reach this point of development. How long have you been in business?" I tried not to appear lacking in empathy, or make my diversions too obvious or too abrupt, but rather connected to the inquiry. I wanted the interviewee to intentionally switch off the emotion about the police and begin thinking clearly about the details of the crime.

Diversion questions may help you to develop and strengthen rapport when you use them to indicate that you have investigated similar matters with similar interviewees. When I announce that many victims feel violated and confused, the interviewee realizes that I have insight into the feelings of victims. In one of my investigations in which a woman received sexually explicit letters, she wondered what she had done to cause the man to send the letters. "How did I lead him on?" she wondered out loud. I tried to reassure her that she was probably at the wrong place at the wrong time and she didn't do anything to deserve or provoke those letters. Diversion questions usually help diffuse a tense situation.

Leading Questions Leading questions include some assumption on the part of the investigator. For example, the statement "From what you say, you must have had a rough time in that job last summer" contains an assumption and invites the interviewee to elaborate or explain. Leading questions containing implicit messages can be used to maintain a moderate emotional tension in the interview, but they need not be abrasive if thoughtfully constructed, as in, "You are under a lot of strain at home, aren't you?" or, "You're not the kind of person that would use that missing money for drugs, are you?" Leading questions are usually thought to produce invalid, unreliable answers. This is true when poorly used. When, however, they are used to build rapport and communicate your understanding and acceptance, leading questions stimulate dialogue and encourage cooperation. They exhibit your assumption that the interviewee can and will provide truthful information.

TECHNIQUES FOR EFFECTIVE QUESTIONING
Having the Gall to Ask

First of all, let's openly recognize that some people do dumb, foolish, hurtful, and dangerous things. Once you accept that, in fact, people do steal from employers and do sexually molest children, then you can see how important it is to ask questions of victims, witnesses, and suspects that are not typical of polite social communication. Investigators "usually have problems asking tough or embarrassing questions and they may even avoid asking these questions to save themselves from embarrassment. There is no doubt it takes a certain amount of gall to ask someone if he or she stole the money, killed the husband, or got drunk and ran over a neighbor's child" (Downs et al., p. 288). Conducting an investigative inquiry requires that you be brave enough to ask questions that would be rude and intrusive in other situations. To justify asking certain questions, all parties must come to realize that those questions are necessary.

Encouraging Cooperation

Although most interviewees feel a personal obligation to answer questions truthfully, that obligation is lessened when the investigator is obviously unskilled in formulating questions. If the interviewer's questioning pattern conflicts with the interviewee's expectations, the interviewee may become frustrated and annoyed. As a consequence, rapport may suffer (Binder and Price). You can encourage cooperation by first asking simple, closed questions that invite a positive response, before moving on to more complex, specific, open questions. By communicating that you need and expect additional facts, you subtly encourage the interviewee to reveal more information (see Chapter 3 and the Self-Fulfilling Prophecy). If you can do so without creating unnecessary tension, imply that you have already obtained considerable information that will provide a context for (and against which you will check) the interviewee's responses. Persuade the interviewee to cooperate with the investigation.

Gain information by strengthening the interviewee's sense of obligation. If necessary, help the interviewee temporarily create a new identity that will allow him or her to move from a position of limited to more complete cooperation. During some interviews I have heard, "I'm not the kind of person to rat on a friend, even if I knew something." Such comments clearly indicate that the interviewee's loyalty to a friend is a significant part of his or her self-image. Therefore it is my job to encourage these interviewees to modifying their stance and fit cooperation into their concept of being a loyal friend. Employees of victim companies that have suffered a theft may initially feel a primary loyalty to their colleagues. When I suggest that they also owe loyalty to the company that provides their livelihood, they often come to understand that finding the thief is best for everyone. Through your properly phrased questions, sell the interviewee on the idea of telling the truth.

Mentally Assuming an Affirmative Answer

To avoid receiving negative responses that lead you to a dead end, mentally assume an affirmative answer to a closed question, and ask the next logical question instead. For example, don't ask, "Have you seen or talked with Sam Smith recently?" The interviewee could easily define recently as within "the last two hours" and answer no, closing off further discussion. Instead, assume that the interviewee has spoken to Smith recently, and ask, "When was the last time you saw or talked with Sam Smith?" This second question, an open question, cannot be answered yes or no. The interviewee must give a full response if he or she answers at all. The response you receive will help determine the direction of subsequent questions. For example, if the interviewee responds, "I spoke with Sam two days ago," you might ask, "What was Sam wearing when you last saw him? What kind of car was he driving? Who was he hanging around with?" These questions will help you determine his appearance, means of transportation, and current associates.

Pursuing Unanswered Questions

There are many reasons why an interviewee might fail to answer a question or might provide an incomplete or nonsensical response. Perhaps the interviewee is preoccupied or distracted and did not hear the question correctly, or perhaps is too overwhelmed by emotion to answer. If your question was poorly worded, the interviewee might not have understood what you were asking. Be patient. Allow the interviewee time to think without challenging him or her. Then ask the question again, varying the wording if appropriate. Never ignore an unanswered question and go on to another topic. To move on and leave questions unanswered will only cause you eventual frustration. When repeating a question, look and listen for signs of deception (see Chapter 1). The interviewee might have something to hide. Always maintain a certain amount of unexpressed skepticism. Be aware of patterns indicating that the truth is emerging.

On the other hand, perhaps by not answering, the interviewee hopes to avoid discussion of a difficult topic. To repeat or reword questions reduces tension during an interview. When the interview touches on sensitive or threatening topics, you may need to repeat or rephrase questions to find a more acceptable form. Some words trigger mental images that may be emotionally painful to the interviewee, causing him or her to block out certain thoughts. Whether you repeat or reword a question depends on the circumstances and how you evaluate your progress in the interview. There are times when it is useful to ask a mild, modified version of an emotionally loaded question before asking the main question. This warns the interviewee of the upcoming emotional question, helping him or her prepare for it. In other cases, it's necessary to spring emotion-laden questions on the interviewee in order to reveal any hidden tension.

Never demand an answer to your question. Don't point out that the interviewee failed to answer. Instead, reword the question and try again. Some interviewees will try to provoke you into challenging them so that they will feel justified in storming out of the interview room. Even victims and witnesses of a crime may feel insulted if challenged by a demand for an answer to a question. By calmly repeating your questions, you signal persistence, patience, and humanity, which strengthen the bonds of interpersonal communication.

Identifying and Challenging Deception

A lead-in that introduces a change of topic—for example, "I'm now going to ask you a few questions about the day the money was missing"—causes some interviewees to nonverbally signal their intent to deceive. They may fidget in their chair, cross their legs or arms, or break eye contact. Any sudden uneasiness should cause you to internally question the truthfulness of the answers that follow. Ask your question, and take note of the interviewee's uneasiness when you evaluate the answer. Throughout the interview, look for patterns that may indicate deception. When a clear pattern of evasiveness becomes evident, gradually challenge the interviewee.

Some degree of unprovoked anxiety may be useful in an interview. You can enhance tension through your use of questions or by commenting on the interviewee's defense mechanisms and sensitivity to certain topics. However, thoughtless confrontation over conflicting details in the interviewee's story could provoke silence. Excessive levels of tension can lean to obstructionist behavior and an unproductive interview.

Handling Trial Balloons

Interviewees sometimes ask "trial balloon" questions that can be difficult to handle. They might ask, "Just say I did steal the money. What would happen to me?" or, "What usually happens to an employee who steals merchandise?" These what-if questions may indicate that the interviewee is on the brink of reporting a significant fact. When the interviewee floats a trial balloon, avoid pouncing and the possibility of an admission of guilt. Instead, calmly respond and ask questions that will encourage the interviewee to tell the truth. Interviewees use what-if questions to test the water, to see if it is safe. These questions signal the need for continued patience and persistence; they do not imply that it is time to charge ahead destructively.

TERMINATION OF THE INTERVIEW

Always assume that more information is forthcoming and that you need only ask the right questions and give adequate encouragement. Even when it seems you have reached the termination point—when it seems as though all questions have been asked and answered—continue to assume more information is available. You might ask, "What else is there that you can tell me about what happened?" or, "What else should I know about this matter?"

Still, at some point, you will need to terminate the interview (see Chapter 8 on "The Terminal Phase"). You can do this several ways. In most cases, you will not need to speak with the interviewee again. If you have any doubts, you can tell the interviewee that you may contact him or her in the future. You might make an appointment for a second interview and give yourself time to prepare further. You might lead into a confrontation with the interviewee by announcing that you believe there are inconsistencies that must be resolved. Finally, you might lead into a confrontation by announcing your opinion that the interviewee is responsible for the matter under investigation. Your next step is to attempt to gain a confession or admission of guilt.

REVIEW QUESTIONS

Answer the following questions and explain your answers fully.

Question Formulation

1. What is the objective of interviewing?

2. What is a question?

3. Should you ask vague questions?

Phrasing and Presenting Questions

1. Is the interview a conversation or a cross examination?

2. Is it important to ask questions objectively?

3. Can your vocabulary cause interviewee resentment?

4. How can you emphasize your genuine interest during the interviewee?

Principles of Question Formulation

1. Are questions in any way like special codes?

2. Give two examples of closed questions.

3. Give two examples of open questions.

4. How do most open questions begin?

5. What are two things that open questions can help you do?

6. Name three types of open questions and give an example of each.

7. Are pointed questions based on the self-fulfilling prophecy?

8. Can diversion questions help you develop and strengthen rapport?

9. What is one advantage of using leading questions?

Techniques for Effective Questioning

1. How do polite social conversations differ from investigative interviews?

2. Do you need courage to ask some questions?

3. Do most interviewees feel a personal obligation to answer questions truthfully?

4. How does your expectation play a role in gaining truthful information?

5. What does it mean for the investigator to be a persuader?

6. Is it a good idea to assume the interviewee has the information you are seeking?

7. Is it a good idea to ignore unanswered questions and go on with the interview?

8. Might your questions trigger emotions that block an interviewee's ability to respond?

9. What is a trial balloon question and who asks it?

Termination of the Interview

1. After all the obvious questions have been asked and answered, should you assume that the interviewee has more information to provide?

2. How can you lead into a confrontation with the interviewee?

REFERENCES

Banaka, William H. *Training in Depth Interviewing*. New York: Harper and Row, 1971.

Binder, D.A., and S.C. Price. *Legal Interviewing and Counseling*. St. Paul: West, 1977.

Downs, Cal W., G. Paul Smeyak, and Ernest Martin. *Professional Interviewing*. New York: Harper and Row, 1980.

11

The Case of the Stolen Traveler's Checks

The following case illustrates the need for investigators to proceed in a way that is blatantly, obviously, repetitious, but never boring. This chapter has lots of repetition because that is what happens in an investigation. Over and over and over again, I use my interview process. If you become bored with the lack of dancing guys and dolls in the following case report, you are not alone. There is little that flashes and jumps on this screen of life.

You will notice, I'm sure, my use of filter factors (see Chapter 7) as I move through each interaction. Even on the phone I use these essential elements which allow me to observe, evaluate, and assess people's truthfulness. Beyond the repetition and seemingly extraneous details of the case, look for my consistent use of, and concern for, the principles suggested in the body of this text.

Pay particular attention to those times when I recognize that interviewees are not being candid. Notice those times when I pay attention to the seemingly small things that ultimately add up to significant information. Also notice how I communicate with JC's mother on the phone and what significance my comments might take on when she conveys them to JC—how my tone of voice told her that JC was in trouble but that I would work with him to resolve the problem. Also, notice my interaction with JC's buddy and traveling companion, Jeff, who really made the difference in this case by using some friendly persuasion on JC.

The case report that follows illustrates the long-term determination investigators need to solve cases. It gives you an overview of the day-by-day progress of a long investigation that required a shifting strategy. The case is broadly divided into the major phases we discussed in Chapters 7 and 8, but notice that all of the interviews move through the Initial and Primary phases. In the end the strengths of my interview process are repetition, persistence, and flexibility.

THE INITIAL PHASE

This case began, as many of my cases do, with a phone call to my office. I was writing, but I don't really mind suspending my writing for a new case, and this one proved to be a real challenge that lasted three months. I didn't work on it every day, of course, but thirty investigative days spread over three months.

"May I speak with Charles Yeschke, please?" a voice inquired over the phone.

"Yes, this is Mr. Yeschke."

"You're the private investigator?"

"Yes."

Doris C. identified herself as the operations officer of a medium-sized bank. She said that she had been referred by a former client of mine. "He spoke highly of you," she said.

"I appreciate the referral. How can I help you?" I asked.

"We had $2,500 in traveler's checks cashed in Las Vegas, but we didn't sell them to anyone. We haven't been able to find out how those checks got out of our bank. We know who cashed them, but we didn't sell them to him. Do you work on things like this?"

"Yes, I do. Would you like me to stop by to talk with you this morning?" I asked.

"This afternoon would be better, if you have the time." She gave me the address, and we agreed to meet at her office sometime after three o'clock that afternoon. Thus began another needle-in-a-haystack type case.

That afternoon, Doris gave me the background on the case. Fifty traveler's checks in $50 denominations had been stolen from the box in which they were kept in the drive-in area. All employees who worked in the drive-in area had easy access to the box. In addition, employees who had duties nearby—including proof department personnel, bank officers, and members of the cleaning crew—had access to the box. Against bank policy, some of these employees were known to use the drive-in area as a short-cut between the parking lot and the main area of the bank.

A careful check of the log sheet revealed that the traveler's checks had not been audited since January 15, two months before the loss was discovered. The daily responsibility for monitoring the checks had been overlooked because of the termination of three employees and the promotion of another. The traveler's checks could have been stolen any time within that two-month period.

Doris also filled me in on some of the key personnel. Anna was the head teller in charge of daily accounting for all traveler's checks. JC was the man who had cashed the stolen checks. Jim was the manager of the contract cleaning crew, and Millie was his wife. Jim and Millie lived near JC. Doris provided copies of the $2,500-worth of checks bearing JC's signature and gave me his Minnesota driver's license number. I considered all of these key players, as well as others, to be suspects.

I suggested to Doris that bank employees and members of the cleaning crew be advised that an internal investigation was under way to determine how the checks had been removed from the bank and how this could be prevented in the future. I wanted her to emphasize the positive, forward-looking nature of the inquiry. I wanted everyone to know that I sought cooperation from anyone who had information about the theft, and that anything they shared would remain confidential.

My first task was to contact JC. His mother answered the phone. In a clear, professional tone of voice, I said, "This is Mr. Yeschke. May I talk with JC, please?" She told me he was not there. I carefully modulated my voice and the timing of my delivery to convey a determined but polite request. It was not my intention to provoke anger or fear. I asked, "Would you have him call me, please? I'm a private investigator, and I think he may be able to help me with an investigation I'm working on. He may have some information that could be of assistance." I gave JC's mother my name and spelled it for her. I also provided my telephone number. She told me she might not see JC for some time but would ask him to call me when she saw him.

Within the hour, JC telephoned to say that he would be busy for a couple of days but would be available for an interview two days hence. He was happy to cooperate in any way he could. When I mentioned why I wanted to talk with him, he seemed surprised. He said that he had had no idea that the checks he cashed had been stolen. I made no effort to question him on the phone. His comments about the checks were spontaneous. I told JC that I would call him back to schedule a time for the interview.

My next step was to visit Jim, the manager of the cleaning crew. As Jim opened the door of his trailer home and invited me in, he was most cordial. His friendly conversation and relaxed manner, however, seemed inconsistent with his lack of eye contact. He looked mainly at the floor as he spoke, and would not look at me except for a few brief glances. I told Jim that I was hoping he could provide a list of his employees who might have had access to the traveler's checks. Jim wrote out the names and telephone numbers of the nine people working on his crew at the time when the checks were presumed to have been stolen. Jim declared that neither he nor members of his crew had stolen the checks. He did have some doubts about Bob, a former employee of his, whom he suspected of stealing some money from a purse at the bank. Jim had paid $20 to the owner of the purse to cover the loss and had not employed Bob since then. In his comments about Bob, Jim seemed almost to be reading from a script.

Jim volunteered some additional information. He told me that he was living at his current residence to be near his son who played high school hockey. This comment seemed intended to show that he was a devoted father. He also volunteered that the security at the bank was not good. He said that one time he had noticed that the vault had not been locked as it should have been, and the bank officer in charge of locking the vault had asked that he not tell bank officials about the incident. Jim added that he had seen people passing through the area where the checks were handled and that they could have had access to the checks if the checks had been left out at night. When I asked if Jim knew JC, he said that he waved to JC at Ralph's Bar, but was not close to him. JC and Jim's brother, Gaul, had gone to school together and were friends. Then I began the series of questions that I would ask all of the interviewees.

"If you had anything to do with taking those checks out of the bank, it's important to get this cleared up," I told him. "How do you stand on that? Did you have any part in taking those checks?"

"I have had access to thousands in cash but did not take any at the bank," he responded. "I could have taken handfuls and not been caught, but I didn't. That job is important to me!"

Did he deny the theft? I asked myself. Not at all.

The next day, I met JC at his mother's home, which was located two blocks away from Jim's trailer. We drove in my car to a nearby restaurant, where JC spoke openly about signing and cashing the traveler's checks. He claimed that a woman named Cathy had given him the checks in Las Vegas and had asked if he would cash them for her. He had gone to Vegas with his friend Jeff, but he did not recall the dates of the trip. He had wanted to find a job there, and Jeff had gone to party. He offered to show me the airline ticket receipts that he had saved; these would show the dates of the trip. His offer seemed to be intended to show his willingness to cooperate with the inquiry. JC's mention of his friend Jeff brought him into the case. He would later play a significant role.

"We went directly to the bar at the Frontier when we got into Vegas," JC said. "Two women approached us. They were probably hookers. Jeff didn't seem interested in the one that came up to him, and before long that one drifted off. I think he was too drunk. I hooked up with Cathy, the other one. I talked with her for a while, and she asked me, 'Are you looking for action? Do you want to make some money?' I said, 'Sure am.' She told me she was separated from her old man, and that she had some traveler's checks that were legal but she didn't have proper identification with her to cash them. I agreed to help her cash the checks, and she said we would party with the money."

In response to my questions, JC described Cathy: 5'8" tall, shoulder-length blond hair, mid-thirties, 130 to 140 pounds, glasses. Her blond hair was straight with some wave. She had worn the same jeans and blouse during her four days in Vegas with JC. Her blouse may have been red. She had worn underpants but no bra, JC recalled. He couldn't recall the color of her panties. He couldn't recall if she had carried a purse. She had had no luggage or identification that he knew of. She had darker color skin, like a good tan. She had no scars or tattoos that he had noticed.

JC said that he thought Cathy lived in Bloomington, a suburb of Minneapolis. He didn't know her phone number or address. He told me that she had snorted coke frequently in the bathroom and offered him some a couple of times, but he declined. According to JC, Cathy had spent $600 to $700 during those four days. She had stood 'right there' behind him as he had cashed the checks. He had given her the money immediately afterward. He had signed a batch of checks at a time. He had never used traveler's checks before. They had had sexual intercourse one time, and had spent most of their time playing the slot machines. She hadn't seemed to eat during all the time he was with her. She wore her glasses infrequently, but she had had them on when they first met. She had no accent when she spoke. He recalled no time when they sat and talked. He hadn't learned any of her views, complaints, or insights. Cathy had not stayed with him at night; she may have stayed at the Frontier Hotel while he and Jeff had stayed at the Hacienda Casino. She had left him periodically without telling him where she was going. As though to reassure me of his innocent participation in the check passing, JC declared, "I wouldn't be dumb enough to cash those checks if I had known they were stolen! I used my ID and all! I could get a false driver's license with my picture on it if I wanted to. I thought the checks were okay. When one place put a check on them to see if they were okay, and they were, then I thought they were okay!"

Before leaving the restaurant, JC agreed to provide the airline ticket receipts and to call me with Jeff's telephone number. He also gave me a telephone number where he could be reached when he was not at his mother's home. I told him I would be in touch in a few days. Then I drove him back to his mother's. I didn't challenge JC's story at all. Through my nonverbal behavior, I tried to signal my neutral position. I wanted him to think that he had provided a smooth, believable story and had nothing to fear. In truth, I was skeptical. He seemed off-course in parts of his narrative, and his failure to remember certain details troubled me. I asked myself, if I were with someone for four days and spending her money, wouldn't I remember more details? But then, he had probably been drunk much of the time in Vegas, and certainly he hadn't been thinking clearly. He did sound fairly convincing, I thought. Still, although JC's story seemed complete, it lacked the free-flowing character needed to convince me. For the time being, I would reserve my opinion.

I began to devote some energy to identifying the woman named Cathy. Georgia, an administrative assistant at the bank, told me that she and seven others had gone to Las Vegas to gamble about a month before the traveler's checks had been cashed. With current and former employees frequenting Las Vegas, there was a real chance that the mysterious Cathy was in some way connected to the bank. Part of the puzzle was how the checks had been taken out of the bank. Perhaps a bank employee had stolen them and gone to Vegas to party. With this new possibility in hand, Cathy took on a new dimension—as did JC's story. I described the mystery woman to Georgia, in the hope that she might be able to identify her. She couldn't think of any current or former bank employee who matched Cathy's description. None of the women was 5'8" tall.

During a phone conversation with Jim, he told me that he had warned everyone on his cleaning crew that he would not stand for anyone stealing from the bank. He said, "I used some hot words with them over the loss of those checks. I talked to JC at Ralph's Bar about the checks, but I wasn't going to get into a fight over them. JC told me to get lost." Jim also gave me the names of two employees on his cleaning crew who had noticed a teller's coin box left out overnight at the bank, and had reported it the following day to bank officials. I asked him who routinely vacuumed the bank vault area. Jim said that he and Tom usually took care of that job. When I told Jim that the bank had lost $20 and $50 on separate occasions from the coin machine in the coin-counting area, he disclaimed any knowledge of the losses.

During Day 3 of the inquiry, I phoned Jim, but he said he hadn't learned anything more about the loss. He lacked the enthusiasm I expected of the head of a cleaning crew whose members were under suspicion for theft. He didn't seem to be making enough waves. When I asked Jim about the whereabouts of his brother, Gaul, he seemed evasive and said that he was not sure where Gaul was. He spoke with hesitation, as though he were holding back information. He said that his brother was "a shaky character" and had had several scrapes with the law in the past. I didn't press for additional information about Gaul because Jim declared that Gaul hadn't worked on the cleaning crew in the bank for at least six months before the checks were believed to have been stolen. He said that Gaul had not had access to the bank during those six months and could not have been involved in the loss. I got the sense that Jim was trying to steer me away from Gaul.

The next day, I tried unsuccessfully to reach JC at the telephone number he had provided. The man who answered the phone told me that JC was in Florida but would return to Minnesota in a few days. I asked that JC contact me upon his return and left my name. JC eventually called and gave me his friend Jeff's address and telephone number, and reiterated his willingness to cooperate with the investigation. He implied that he was embarrassed to be caught up in the inquiry and that he was an innocent party in the passing of stolen checks. He agreed to meet me again to discuss the matter.

I called Jeff at his place of employment and received confirmation of JC's account of the trip to Las Vegas. Jeff had gotten the cash for the trip from JC who owed him money. He told me that while at the Frontier Hotel bar, he and JC had met two women who were in their mid-thirties. The women had said they were also from Minneapolis. Jeff had not heard their names. He claimed to be "blasted" at the time and unable to recall anything well. JC had gone off with one of the women, but Jeff had had no interest in the other, and she had left shortly thereafter. He and JC had planned to spend only a day or so in Vegas, but they had stayed on from Tuesday to Saturday. He had called his employer in Minneapolis to get more time off. Jeff thought that he had heard the woman with JC say something about "making some money," but he couldn't be sure how it was said. She had said something about breaking up with her old man and not having "money or ID." She had been "decent looking" with light hair, may have worn jeans but had not worn glasses. Once she and JC had left the bar, he hadn't seen her again. Jeff named three bars where JC hung out in the Minneapolis area, and he agreed to meet with me for another discussion regarding this matter. Jeff was gainfully employed and his narrative about the Las Vegas trip seemed to flow. I considered him cooperative and probably truthful. He was not in a hurry to terminate the conversation, and he was willing to discuss the matter again. Of course, phone interviews leave a lot to be desired. Over the phone, you can't see the nonverbal signals that play the biggest part in determining whether an interviewee is being honest.

I telephoned Bob, a former cleaning crew member, at the number Jim had given me. Jim had told me that, of all the people who had worked on his crew, Bob was the most likely to have stolen from the bank. I questioned Bob about his access to the bank. He told me that he had not been in the bank at any time during the two months before the theft was discovered. The previous fall, he had cleaned some windows for Jim at the bank; he had also cleaned windows last week but had not yet been paid for that work. He told me that about two weeks earlier, he had stopped by the bank to get a ride from Jim. He had knocked on the window, and Millie had let him in. Jim had given him a ride home after buying him dinner. After my usual preamble, I asked Bob outright if he had stolen the traveler's checks.

"No, I didn't!" he declared.

"Do you know who did take them?"

"No!"

"Well, then, who do you think might be involved?" I asked.

"I have no idea!"

Bob said that Jim had introduced him to JC about three years before at Ralph's Bar where Jim and JC used to hang out together.

Bob's information certainly didn't solve the investigative problem, but it did shed some light on the overall accessibility of unauthorized people to the bank. He had also given me something to think about regarding the relationship between Jim and JC. Before beginning more interviews on Day 5 of the investigation, I reviewed my information about how JC had cashed the checks in Las Vegas. The check cashing spree had been an open and bold action during which there may have been video coverage of JC signing the checks. I was building my strategy for when I would talk with JC again. Official records showed that $1,800 of the $2,500 in stolen checks were cashed at the following establishments:

The Golden Gate	5 checks
Hacienda Casino	5 checks
Desert Inn	3 checks
Frontier Hotel	5 checks
Stardust Hotel	3 checks
Aladdin Hotel	4 checks
Westward Ho Hotel	10 checks

I telephoned JC again. He told me that he had "just rolled into town" and would call me when he got settled. His remarks sounded like a polite put-off. His behavior suggested he was trying to avoid me, and I wondered why.

I reviewed the progress of the investigation with Anna, the head teller. She named a bank employee with long blond hair who had gone to Las Vegas with seven other bank employees two months before the theft was discovered. I gave Anna JC's description of Cathy and asked her to pass it along the bank employees' grapevine. Perhaps it would spark some additional information. Anna also told me that people who had attended night classes at the bank might have had access to the drive-in area. Outsiders could have wandered into that area if the cleaning people had propped open certain doors as they worked. Great! I thought. More leads to track down.

THE PRIMARY PHASE

I reviewed the progress of the investigation with Doris. I told her that if the checks had not been locked up according to bank policy, it appeared that many people might have had access to them.

Doris recalled that, at Jim's request, Gaul had fixed a water cooler in the bank.

On the phone once again, Jim recalled that Bob, looking for a ride, had stopped in at the bank about three weeks earlier. In a later conversation, Jim told me that Gaul ran from woman to woman and had been married six times. He told me that JC had two children, that Gaul had once had an affair with JC's wife, and that JC probably held hard feelings toward Gaul. None of Jim's friends socialized with JC. He told me that Gaul had never been in the new bank building, although he had been in the old bank building some time in the past. Gaul had spent time in two different jails and had been arrested many times for traffic violations and other minor things. Jim reminded me about the bank officer who had forgotten to lock the vault one night and had asked him not to report it. Before ending this interview, Jim volunteered, "If JC had known the checks were stolen, he wouldn't have used his real name!" Of course, these were almost the exact words JC had used to explain his involvement in cashing the checks. I responded that it was reasonable to assume that JC wouldn't intentionally get himself into trouble. It appeared that Jim was identifying with the potential thief. A logic of sorts?

In an attempt to locate and interview Barb, who had once worked at the bank, I contacted her former roommate, Jackie, another former bank employee. She named several bars that Barb frequented, and described how Barb's lifestyle had changed recently. Barb now hung out with a music band and dated one of the players. She gave me the name of a woman with whom Barb had lived for a month after she and Jackie had broken off their friendship. She did not think of Barb as the type of person who would steal from the bank, even though she had had a problem with the bank and had either been fired or quit. Although she did not like Barb, Jackie declared that she trusted her. She provided Barb's new address and telephone number.

During Day 6 of the inquiry, Anna told me that the information about the traveler's checks having been cashed in Vegas had flowed through the bank's grapevine. All of the employees seemed to be thinking about what had happened and who might have been involved. Amy, a cleaning crew worker, declared that she had worked for Jim five or six times, doing some dusting in the bank. She had never heard of JC, but she told me that Gaul, Jim's brother, was said to be in jail. She named several former employees of Jim's who had worked in the bank.

Sometimes I find it helpful to stir the investigative pot a little to see what floats to the top. I decided to pay particular attention to Jeff to see if, through him, I couldn't influence JC's cooperation. I intended to direct my energies and attention so that, even though I didn't explicitly say it, Jeff would understand he was being singled out as a co-conspirator. I tried to reach Jeff by phone, but he wasn't home. The woman who answered the call said that Jeff was not yet home from work, and that he went to work at about eight o'clock each morning.

I caught up with Barb the next day. She had a male friend with her as I arrived at her home for our scheduled appointment. The two of them were seated on a screened-in porch when I arrived. He sat in on the beginning of my interview with Barb, as though observing me and how I treated her. After a few minutes, he said something to her about car repairs and left us. Barb gave me a clear account of how the bank opened for business every day when she worked there. She was convinced that the cleaning crew had never entered drive-in area until everything was locked up properly. Although she had been considered a nonconformist by some at the bank, she seemed proud of the way everyone had followed bank policy in locking up at the close of business. She recalled that checks had been accounted for by number, and someone had been assigned the duty of replenishing the checks when they were depleted. She seemed concerned over the loss and expressed a willingness to cooperate in the inquiry. When I asked her directly whether she had any part in removing the checks from the bank, she replied, "No I didn't! Do they think that I took them?" She sounded disgusted with the bank and disappointed that anyone would think she might be involved in the theft. In an effort to soothe her, I said, "There's nothing to indicate you are the one who did it." She calmed as quickly as she had flared up. I asked whether she would mind taking a polygraph examination, and she agreed if it would assist in the investigation. She said, "I have nothing to hide because I wasn't involved in taking those checks."

My next interview was with Mary Kay, another former bank employee. She had had access to the checks just before quitting her job because of a personality clash with someone in management. In response to my direct questions, she denied being involved in the theft and said that she didn't know who was responsible. When I asked whom she suspected, she had a number of suggestions.

"Barb ran with a bad sort," she told me. "She moved to Texas. Then there's Jean, who was on probation for being over and 'short' in her working cash. I just don't know for sure who stole those checks. Maybe the janitors did it. There was a time when I was out sick and I left my coin [box] out. The next day I was short $20 in coin. The janitors had access to the coin, but I don't know for sure. People on that cleaning crew come in high or drunk at times. I saw some of them coming out of a bar near the bank on their way to work. Nancy was in charge of the checks, and they were normally balanced each Wednesday. Anna was the one who arranged to have large additions made to the working amount of checks as it was depleted. Anna and the vault teller moved a supply of the checks from the vault to the box used by the tellers on a daily basis." Mary Kay added, "Jim bragged a lot and made a play for the girls!" Mary Kay declared her willingness to undergo a polygraph examination. She denied knowing JC or anything about the checks being cashed in Las Vegas. She suggested that she check with one of her friends who knew several bank employees. He might know of some connection between JC and a bank employee. A couple of days later, Mary Kay phoned to report that she had checked with her friend, but he had no information.

I tried to get in touch with JC and spoke with his mother again. She said that JC had been at her house the day before but was now at his permanent residence about one hundred miles away. I asked her to pass along a message to JC—that I would like to talk with him in the near future. I again gave her my name and telephone number. I was polite in making my request, hoping that she would report my professional demeanor and determined manner to JC

Tracy, the vault teller, declared that, at times, the checks had not been locked up in the vault as required by policy, but had been left out overnight. She suspected the janitors of stealing money from the bank. If the checks had not been put in the vault and the cleaning crew had had access while vacuuming, they could have stolen them, she thought. A month or so before the loss of the checks had been noticed, rolls of coins had been missing from a teller's coin vault near where the checks were taken. She also reported having seen one of the young cleaning crew members drinking in a parked car in the bank parking lot. She reported that no one had had the specific duty to oversee the checks other than to replenish them when they were low. They were replenished as needed from bulk storage.

"Tracy, as I've mentioned, I want to find out who took those checks out of the bank," I told her. "If you had anything to do with it, it's important that you tell me about it. How do you stand on that? Did you have anything to do with getting those checks out of the bank?"

"No!" she said.

"Well then, do you know who did take those checks out of the bank?"

"No!"

"Who do you think might be involved, because of what they did or said, even though you don't know for sure?"

"The janitors!"

"Of all the people who had access to the checks, whom do you trust the most? Who, do you feel, would not have taken those checks?"

"The tellers!" she said. The she added, "Jim went to Hawaii. There are too many young kids on that cleaning crew. There was one janitor who stared at the money."

"What else can you tell me about the cleaners?"

"They go through everyone's desk."

Tracy responded throughout her interview in an open, clear thinking, and smooth-flowing way. She seemed pleased to cooperate, and she gave each question some thought. She did not duck or dodge any questions during the inquiry.

On Day 10 of the investigation, Bill stopped at the door of the bank-office-turned-interview-room, asking, "Is this the place I should be for my interview?"

"Yes," I said, introducing myself. "Please come in and have a seat here." Bill had been employed as a bank officer for only a short time before the loss of the checks. He told me that from time to time, as a closing procedure and when assigned to do so, he checked all drawers and the vault. He would not have had contact with the checks in the normal course of business. From time to time, though, he used certain equipment in the drive-in teller area.

"Who would have access to the area if things were left out?" I asked.

"If something is left out, the cleaning crew could get to it."

"Do you know of any time when anything of value was left out?"

"Oh, sure. In my first four months at the bank, a teller left early and forgot to lock up her coins."

"Do you know if any of the coins was missing?"

"I'm not sure. Everyone discussed it," he said. "Her coin box was left out, but it was covered. I do think there was coin missing."

He spoke self-consciously, with poor eye contact. I asked whether he knew the area in which JC and Jim lived.

"No, I don't!" he replied.

"Who do you suspect of taking those checks?"

"Barb and Mary Kay!" This he said in a crisp, clear manner with easy eye contact. Overall, Bill appeared to be somewhat uneasy during the interview, as though he were holding back some information. His answers sounded studied rather than spontaneous. His verbal and nonverbal communication did not properly connect or flow smoothly. He appeared anxious.

In my interview with Nancy, she told me that, before becoming the head teller, she had been accountable for the automatic teller machine (ATM) and the checks.

"Would you help me understand how the checks have been handled over the past few months?" I asked. With this request, Nancy entered into what I call an emotional dumping process. She let loose a flood of information.

"The closing tellers put things away at closing time after they have removed the key to the signature machine and put it into the box containing the checks. When Mary Kay was terminated from the bank, I took her job as head teller. With that move, Suanne became responsible for the ATM and the checks. I don't know of any time the checks were left out improperly. I've been busy with my new job and may not have instructed Suanne completely in how to monitor the checks on a weekly basis. The longest time the checks went unmonitored was probably two weeks." Nancy seemed self-conscious in her comments, somewhat defensive, and maybe even apologetic. She seemed to be struggling with the pressures of her new responsibilities and, perhaps, guilt because she had not properly instructed Suanne in handling the checks.

"Nancy, I'm asking everyone about the same things to try to figure out how those checks were removed from the bank. I'm trying to fit together some pieces to the puzzle. I'd like you to share with me some of your views on this matter," I began. Then I asked her directly whether she was responsible for the theft.

"No!" she declared.

Did she know who took the checks?

"No, I can't imagine!"

"Who does she trust the most?"

"I trust all of the tellers, I have complete trust in all of them!"

"Who does she suspect?"

"I hate to be a judge, but the janitors are in there. A few months ago coin was missing from a coin vault, about $50 worth. That vault has a tricky lock on it, and it caught some times!"

"Have you ever noticed any time when the checks were left out?"

"From the beginning of my new job I've come in early, and I haven't noticed the checks left out overnight. The tellers have never mentioned to me that the checks were left out!" The reference, "from the beginning of my new job," seemed too specific. She didn't say that she did or didn't know the checks had been left out. She seemed evasive.

"Do you have any suspicions of any tellers or bank officers that might be involved in removing those checks?"

"No!"

"Well, I thank you for your comments. I'll continue to look for more information. I appreciate your sharing your thoughts with me. I have to assume that someone walked off with those checks, and I'd like to determine how that happened so that we can prevent it's happening in the future. Thank you for your time. I'll let you get back to work again."

"I'm sorry I wasn't much help to you, but I really don't know how it happened!"

"You have been helpful. I appreciate what you shared with me," I assured her.

In my interview with Suanne, she told me, "Anybody could have walked off with those checks. The checks were lost four months prior to being reported stolen. They should have been audited each month. The first time I learned how to audit the checks was two months before the loss was discovered. I feel bad about the loss and not checking as I should have."

I asked directly whether she had stolen the checks.

"No!"

Did she know who did?

"No! I only balanced the receipts for the sale of the checks and did not completely check or validate the checks."

Who did she suspect?

"I couldn't name anyone. I trust them all! All of the tellers put things away, including the checks. It's not the sole duty of only one person. The box containing the checks was always closed."

"Do you know of anyone under any pressure at the bank?" I asked.

"No."

"Who might have hung around the drive-in area?"

"No one. The personal bankers help in the closing process."

"Have the checks ever been left out overnight?"

"No, never to my knowledge. In the past, a coin vault was left open, and some coin was missing."

"What else can you tell me about those checks and how they were handled?" I asked Suanne.

"The checks always had a rubber band around them when in that box," she said. "When I took over, they may already have been missing from the box! I never got any of the checks out of bulk storage. It took two people to do that."

Georgia stopped me in the hallway of the bank to talk. She said that her daughter had sold a car to Gaul, who had then re-sold the car and title. Gaul had gone to jail for those sales or for some other matter, Georgia said. Her daughter knew a neighbor who was a friend of Gaul's, and the neighbor had arranged the car sale. Her daughter didn't know Gaul otherwise.

It became clear to me that I was grasping for anything that might help me solve this case. With so many people who might have been involved and with the weak bank security procedure, I hoped for heavenly intervention. I phoned Jeff at his place of employment, and we made an appointment for an interview the next evening at a coffee shop near his home. I couldn't be sure of how loyal Jeff was to his friend, JC. He didn't seem to be a strong supporter, nor did he seem to be trying to sell me on the story. How might I play Jeff to gain JC's attention? Jeff hadn't seemed calculating when reporting what he knew about the checks. Our interview would have to be all moment-to-moment maneuvering—nothing specific planned. Jeff and I ordered coffee and settled into the booth. He knew why he was there, so I didn't think it necessary to give a preamble into my questions. He seemed somewhat inconvenienced by the interview. Although tolerant of my efforts, he seemed to convey that he thought himself removed from the investigation, not part of it.

"Please tell me, what do you know about the checks cashed by JC in Vegas?" I asked Jeff.

"I was at Ralph's Bar on Monday night when JC came in and suggested he and I go to Vegas for a day or two and party. I didn't have any money for the trip, so JC repaid me money he owed me. The next day, he and I went to Vegas. We went to the Frontier Hotel after checking into the Hacienda. At the Frontier, we were at the bar a short time when two women came up to talk to us. They were probably hookers. I was drunk at the time and didn't pay that much attention to what was going on. I couldn't hear what was being said by the woman with JC before they left together. The other woman and I were at the bar for a short time before she left me alone there. I didn't see JC again until Friday night when he and I partied. We slept at the Hacienda and took the rental car back on Saturday before taking the plane home that morning. JC paid for the rental car. I gave him $25 when we first rented the car. We took the limousine from the rental place to the airport. JC also paid for the room on Saturday, but I wasn't with him when he did that. In the plane on the way home JC told me about the woman's approach to him that first day at the bar. JC said that she gave him a handful of money for helping her cash some checks. Because she had broken up with her husband, she told JC, she didn't have proper identification, and asked him to cash the checks for her. It was late Tuesday or early Wednesday that JC left a note for me saying that we were returning home on Saturday. We were, to begin with, only going to stay in Vegas for a day or so. I had to call my boss to ask if it was okay for me to take those extra days off, and he said okay.

"I didn't see any checks. All I know, really, is what JC told me happened. Most of the time I was smashed. We were at that bar with those women for about half an hour before JC left with one of them. I remember their asking us where we were from, but nothing else is clear to me." I explained to Jeff that the bank might decide to prosecute and that he might need an attorney, which could be costly.

"That's bull - - - -!" he exclaimed. "I didn't do anything with those checks! All I know is what JC told me. I didn't get any of the money! I don't see why I have to worry about anything or get an attorney!"

I pointed out to Jeff that he had benefited indirectly from the stolen checks because JC had probably paid for the rental car and the hotel room with some of the money from the checks.

"Well, what does JC say about the checks and how he got them?" Jeff wanted to know.

"There are inconsistencies in JC's story. There are too many coincidences surrounding those checks. I'm uncomfortable with what I'm finding out to this point. I don't think that JC is being completely truthful, and, as I see it, that puts you in the middle. I hope you see what I'm trying to say to you, Jeff. It looks like you will need some legal advice on this thing, and an attorney probably won't touch it until you put a few thousand dollars up front."

"Well, I didn't have anything to do with stealing or cashing those checks," Jeff said. "At this stage in my life, I can't stand any problems. I got myself a good woman now, and I'm at a solid job. I can't afford to get an attorney or have any trouble like this."

"I want you to know, Jeff, that I don't think that you personally were involved in handling those checks, but you can see that you did profit from the theft. I'm sure it will all be resolved, but in the process it looks like you may have to defend yourself by getting an attorney, which will cost you some money, time, and embarrassment.

"I hope that JC will be able to clear this up," I continued, "and I hope that it can all be resolved without causing you any trouble. Please keep in mind that I don't consider you involved in the theft of the checks at this time. Maybe you and JC could discuss this, and he can talk with me again to give me some true facts. I'd like to resolve this as soon as possible. The bank needs to make a decision on what to do. They can handle it quietly, or they can take it to the legal authorities for court action. I have recommended that they hold off for a while to give people a chance to tell the truth."

"Well, I think JC should come across if he needs to. I don't like being in this situation!" Jeff exclaimed. He was not a happy guy. I could see his anger welling up, first toward the bank and then toward JC, his buddy. I hadn't known until then how significant Jeff would be to my investigation. I wanted to create dissension between Jeff and JC in order to get some answers. Jeff might not be smarter than JC, but he was certainly bigger, and bigger was definitely better in this case. JC knew that I couldn't really force him to spill the information I needed, but perhaps his buddy Jeff could.

"I'm going to let you think about this and maybe talk to JC," I said. "I'm convinced he has not been straight with me. There is no reason for you to be in this situation when you didn't know anything about those checks to begin with." As Jeff got up to leave, he had a determined look on his face—that concentrated look of a man who has been taken advantage of, who realizes that he has been used by someone he trusted, and has a mission. "I'll be talking to JC about this!" he said.

"I hope JC will get this straightened out soon because the bank needs to make a decision," I reminded him.

After Jeff left, I completed the notes I had taken during the interview so that I could recreate the conversation later. It's my policy to review my notes immediately after an interview so I don't forget what happened. Generally, I travel only about a block or so before stopping to change my hieroglyphics into complete sentences. If I wait for a half hour before I recreate my notes, I'm sure to lose some details I may need.

THE TERMINAL PHASE

I finally reached JC by telephone at his mother's house on Day 12 of the traveler's check inquiry. He said that he had been at his mother's for the past two days and had meant to call me.

"There are many things in this case that seem coincidental and that I'm uncomfortable with," I said, "such things as Cathy living in Minneapolis, your mother residing a few blocks from Jim, and Jim cleaning the bank. My main concern is how those checks got out of that bank."

"I don't know who took them out of the bank!" he declared.

Yes, that may be true, I thought, but you certainly know who handed those checks to you and under what conditions.

"Have you had any contact with Jim to discuss this thing?" I asked.

"I don't know where Jim lives. I tried to locate him but couldn't."

"I know that you have associated with Jim at Ralph's Bar in the past, and he lives about two blocks from your mom!" I said. I wanted to give JC the impression that I thought he was a liar—without calling him one. He had to have sensed that I didn't buy his story and that I was determined to discover the truth. I wasn't going away. "I'd really like to talk to you about this thing to get it straightened out," I told JC.

"I can meet you tomorrow about seven to talk it over," he said.

"That's fine, I replied, in a matter-of-fact way. "I'll be over to take you to coffee then. I want you to know that, based on some information I've developed, the story you have given me is incorrect!"

"I really did meet two women in Vegas, and one of them had some checks. I don't know who took those checks out of the bank!" he declared.

I've certainly got his attention, I thought. I said, "I'm sure we can resolve this thing." Then subtly maneuvering, I hoped, I said, "The bank is considering what to do next in this case."

When I arrived at JC's mother's house, a handwritten note hung from the screen door. It said that JC "had to go to the hospital" before my arrival. "Come over in the morning if you can, JC."

The next morning, I telephoned JC and he said that I could talk with him then. I went over immediately, and we sat in the kitchen. JC gave me copies of the airline tickets he and Jeff had used for their trip to Las Vegas. He admitted that he had talked to Jim at his trailer recently, and he wanted to emphasize that what he had told me about the events in Vegas was the complete truth.

I responded, "Well, I want you to know that when I checked certain parts of what you told me, inconsistencies cropped up. You know, in Vegas they take TV shots of people cashing checks. Let's go over a couple of points. You told me that the woman who gave you those checks wore glasses, she had a red blouse, she didn't do much small-talking, her name was Cathy, she lives in the Bloomington suburb of Minneapolis, she had light blond hair, she wore jeans and maybe tennis shoes, she had no purse, she left and did not say good-bye to you, and she probably stayed at the Frontier. Does that about cover the details?"

"You know all there is to know!" he said.

"As long as you're sure you're not holding back anything, I'd like you to take a polygraph examination to verify what you've told me. How do you feel about doing that so we can clear up this confusion?"

"Sure, I'll take one because I'm telling the truth!" he said. "I talked to Jeff about this recently, and he remembers what happened."

I left him with the thought that I would continue the investigation and arrange a polygraph examination for him. I returned to the bank for additional interviews with the staff. During my eighteen-minute conversation with Elsie, she explained that she shared head teller responsibilities with Nancy. She was composed during the interview, and there were no emotional outbursts. She denied stealing the traveler's checks from the bank, and she had no idea who might have been responsible.

Next I interviewed Carol, another bank employee. After the usual preamble, I asked if she had had anything to do with removing the checks from the bank. She said she had not. She could not identify the guilty person and said she suspected no one.

"Who do you trust the most?" I asked her.

"Everyone," she said, "the two head tellers the most!"

"What do you think should happen to the person responsible for the theft?"

"They should pay it back and go to the workhouse!" she declared. "Don't waste tax money! There should be a review of the people who have had large differences over the last year, and they should be questioned about the checks."

The next interview, with Jodie, lasted about fifteen minutes. She denied involvement in the theft and couldn't point a finger at anyone else. Whom did she suspect?

"Nobody," she said. "A lot of people had access. People walk through. Anyone is free to come in that way. The janitors are in there!"

When Mary arrived for her interview, she seemed comfortable with me immediately, as though she had been well-briefed about me before her arrival. She seemed to be an inquisitive individual who had thought over the matter of the missing checks. Without being asked, she blurted out, "JC lives near Tracy the vault teller! According to the head teller, those checks were left out. Nancy told me that!" Later, she told me, "Two months ago, a teller coin vault was left open over two nights, and either $30 or $50 was missing in coin!" She denied that she had stolen the checks, and she said that she trusted everyone in the drive-in area.

I asked, "Has anyone ever asked you to help them steal from the bank, even though you never did?"

"No!" she responded, and then blurted out, "In August or sometime last summer, Tracy lost the vault key. She might have put it into a customer's bank bag!"

I asked her to suggest consequences for the guilty party.

"What should happen to the person who actually did take those checks?" she repeated. She seemed to be contemplating the gravity of the question. Then she said, "Whoever did it should be prosecuted and made to reimburse the bank!"

Lonna seemed comfortable within the first four minutes of her interview, but she did not volunteer any information without being asked. I asked her outright if she was the one who stole the checks. She smiled, looked me right in the eye, and said, "No!"

Who did she suspect?

"We are open seven to seven," she said, "and a lot of people walk around down there!"

I had a short, but definitely not sweet, interview with Kathy. She carried a chip on her shoulder from the very beginning. When I asked her for her date of birth, she thought for a moment before challenging me, "My Social Security number would do just as well as my date of birth!" To reduce her rising anger, I explained, "I ask about date of birth for identification purposes only. Sometimes people have the same name, and I always use the date of birth to keep my records straight. I don't care how old you are." Kathy seemed to resent having to participate in the investigation, as though it were an imposition. Her remarks, although revealing and helpful, did not flow freely. She referred to her coworkers as "ladies," and I took this as a hint about how she wanted to be treated: no lady revealed her age to anyone, especially a stranger, and no lady should be questioned in any way about so crude an event as a theft. With these indicators in mind, I proceeded cautiously to engage her in the interview. She denied any involvement in the theft and couldn't identify the guilty party.

"I can't imagine anyone I work with taking the checks," she said.

"Who do you suspect?" I asked.

"I trust all the ladies I work with!"

"Who had access to those checks?"

"Cleaning people and employees."

"Who do you trust the most?"

"Elsie, if I have to name someone!"

"What should happen to the thief?"

"Well, I imagine they should be prosecuted!"

Two days later, I tried to reach Tom, a member of Jim's cleaning crew, and arrange an interview. His mother answered the phone and told me that Tom would be home from school at about four. I gave her my name and identified myself as a private investigator. "Would you please let Tom know that I called and that I'll call him soon? I asked. "He's not in any trouble. I just want to get his help on a case I'm working. He may have information that could help me."

Several days later, during an interview at her home, Jim's wife Millie said, "Bill, the bank officer, was in a hurry to go to a ball game one night, and he did not check things properly. The vault was not locked as it should have been." Then she said, "The chances are slim that the checks have ever been left out and not locked up! We have a lot to lose by taking those checks. Everybody on the cleaning crew worked the drive-in area of the bank."

I asked her if she stole the checks.

"No, absolutely not. I've taken a crime course in school, and dealing with a bank is like dealing with the government. If there is any question about me, I'm willing to take a lie detector test. I'd put my life on Jim, his son, and me. We didn't do it!" she said. "I think it's someone in the bank, and this is putting a lot of pressure on the cleaning crew."

"Who can you think of as a possible suspect?" I asked.

"Bob is the only one, but he has only worked at the bank three times," she said. Then she said, as though she were trying to figure out an answer to a question she had been considering for a while, "You know, why would JC sign those checks if he knew they were stolen?"

"Are you aware of any time that JC has been here?" I asked.

"Jim has never told me that JC was in this house! JC used to be the chef at Ralph's Bar. You know, I think we'll lose that bank cleaning job no matter what happens in your investigation!"

"Well, it's hard to say how the bank is going to handle this. I suggest we wait to see the outcome. It's too soon to come to any conclusion, I think. Let me ask you, do you think that JC knew that Jim worked at the bank?"

"I think so," she responded.

"Well, I have to be going. Thank you for your cooperation. I'll probably talk with you again. Please tell Jim that I stopped by to talk with you."

At the bank two days later, I interviewed Theresa briefly.

"Theresa, did you have anything to do with removing those checks from the bank?" I asked.

"No!" She said.

"Who, if anyone, do you suspect?"

"The janitors! I had $50 missing in coin, and if they would take coin, they would take checks. The coin was missing a few months ago from my coin vault. It was hard to lock."

"Do you suspect any of your fellow workers of taking those checks?"

"Not a one!"

"Do you know if the checks have ever been left out?"

"I have no idea!" She replied.

Three days went by before JC contacted me by telephone. He said he was on his way out of town and would call me in about two and a half weeks. He would consult with his attorney and might take the polygraph examination.

I told him, "The more I look into this matter, the more holes I see in your story. The bank is going to have to make a move soon in this case!"

"Let's say that someone did give me the checks," he said, "then what?"

"Well, as I've told you before, the main concern is how the checks got out of the bank. The bank wants to prevent it from happening again. They won't profit by prosecuting anyone. My recommendation is going to be to get recovery on the checks and not push for prosecution. I can't answer for the bank, but I believe they will follow my recommendation."

"Does the bank intend to put someone in jail?" he asked, concern evident in his tone.

"As I said, I won't recommend prosecution!"

"When I get back, I might take a polygraph test."

"I'll look forward to your call so we can get this cleared up," I said.

This short conversation convinced me that JC was worried. That same day, the owner of Ralph's Bar told me that JC frequented the bar often and received many personal telephone calls there. He did not know JC's habits and couldn't add more. I hoped that word would get back to JC that I had stopped by the bar to ask questions about him because it would probably make him even more uneasy.

A day or so later, Jean, a bank employee who resembled the description given for the mysterious Cathy, told me everything she knew in a long, rambling monologue. "It might have been someone in debt or someone trying to get revenge or maybe just for the excitement of doing it," she suggested. "The checks were situated near the check encoder. I don't think anyone would take those checks. Maybe they were sold, but no money was taken in." Her remark about no money coming into the bank seems silly—if someone steals traveler's checks, it would defeat their purpose to then pay the bank for them. But under the stress of a personal interview, she wasn't thinking clearly. Many people make illogical comments in the heat of the investigation.

"There were a lot of new tellers at that time," she continued. "There was a part-time worker in there, and some new personal bankers spent the day in the auto bank [the drive-in area]. Two armored car guards routinely go into the vault where the bulk of the checks are stored. Tracy and Nancy take care of replenishing the checks when they run low in the auto bank area."

I asked her the routine questions. She said she didn't do it, she didn't know who did, and she didn't suspect anyone. "Is there anyone who makes you feel uncomfortable because of what they have said or done, who causes you to think they might have been involved in taking those checks out of the bank?" I asked.

"I had a $500 shortage one time! Lorrie, the bank messenger, reaches over my cash to pick up my work, but no one." Again, more comments from a less than calm person. She obviously means she can think of no one person about whom she feels uncomfortable.

"My understanding is that you went to Las Vegas in the past couple of months. Is that correct?"

"I drove to Florida. I've never been to Las Vegas. It would take someone with a lot of guts to take those checks out of the bank and cash them!"

By telephone, Roberta, a former bank employee, told me that she was about to leave for a job interview but would be available to talk to me at about 7:45 that evening. We spoke that evening for twenty-seven minutes. Roberta said that she had decided to leave the bank to start school. She gave me the name and location of her new employer. She had no other information. Although the interview with Roberta might seem useless, it was possible that she might have kept up her friendships with bank employees, might have telephoned one of them about her evening interview, and, thereby, have reported my persistence.

Twenty days later, I tried to contact JC by telephone. His mother promised to ask JC to call me. I caught up with Tom, Jim's employee, that same day. He denied any involvement in the theft.

"I didn't know about the checks until Jim told me about them being missing," he said.

Did he know who had removed them?

"No," he said. "Could they have been put into the trash?"

"It doesn't look like they went into the trash," I said. I named several of the members of the cleaning crew one at a time and asked if they were possible suspects in his mind. He said they were not. Who, then, did he think might have taken those checks?

"No janitors!" he replied.

I tried repeatedly over the next few days to contact JC. His mother dutifully took my messages, but JC never called me back. Finally, I telephoned Jeff to tell him that JC had not returned my calls and seemed to be avoiding me. "Jeff, as I've told you, the bank needs to make a move on this matter. It looks to me like JC's story is full of holes. There is no need for any court action on this if we can find out how it happened, but the bank can only wait so long. It' still possible that you will be able to avoid the financial burden of defending yourself, but at this point, all I can do is hope that JC is willing to talk to me and tells the truth."

"Let me check with JC on this," he said. "Give me a call if he doesn't call you!"

Two days later, JC finally phoned. "JC, I'm glad you called," I told him. "We need to get this cleared up as soon as possible, otherwise the bank is going to have to take some legal action to recover the money. The more I consider the details in this case, the more holes I can see in your story. We really have to revise what you have given me on how this thing went down." He agreed to meet me at a nearby coffee shop.

When JC arrived, he announced that he would not say to anyone else what he was about to say to me. I sat across the table from him without my usual pen and pad. We ordered coffee.

"I got the checks from Jim," he said. "I don't know how they were removed from the bank."

"Thank you for clearing this up. I need to know what happened in more detail."

"I think Jim will deny it!" he said.

"He might, but I need more information so that I'm prepared to talk to him about it. How did Jim make contact with you on the checks? You certainly didn't know they had been removed from the bank unless you took them yourself, and I don't see that happening!"

"Jim approached me in Ralph's and offered me the checks. He said we would split the money from the checks if I would cash them in Vegas. He gave me money for the airfare, and we agreed that I would give him some money from the checks when I returned."

When I asked JC if he would be willing to testify to what he had just told me, he said no. I took a chance with a bluff. I told him, "I'm wired! An associate of mine is out there recording everything we've said! So, there might be a time when you are called to testify on this case. I don't plan for that to happen, but if this can't be straightened out easily through Jim, the bank may ask you to testify about our conversation." My reasoning was that if JC believed I had recorded his admission, and he then told Jim about it, the fact of a recording might encourage Jim to confess his theft.

"I thought this might happen!" JC said. From that point on, JC was reluctant to say anything of significance.

"I'd like you to talk to Jim about what we've discussed and explain the importance of clearing this matter up," I told JC. As he left, he would not promise to talk to Jim as requested. He seemed to be in a daze, not knowing what his next move should be.

The next day, I phoned Jim and Millie's home. Millie said she did not know how to reach Jim. "He's busy on a cleaning job," she said. "What's the big rush to talk to him?"

"I want to arrange for a polygraph examination for him so that we can get this thing resolved as soon as possible!" I told her.

"I'll have him call you as soon as I get hold of him!" she promised.

Jeff called the next day to ask if JC had contacted me to explain his role in the theft. "He did," I said. "It looks like this is finally getting resolved, but it's not complete yet. There's more detail to nail down."

"If you need anything from me, just call," he said. "I didn't have anything to do with those checks!"

That same day, by telephone, Jim declared that he was willing to undergo a polygraph examination. I did not mention to him what JC had told me, and I made no accusations toward him, even though JC had implicated him in the theft of the checks. There was a chance that JC's story was false and that he was trying to put the blame on Jim to get the heat off himself. Also, I didn't want news of JC's accusation to influence the polygraph examination. Jim and I made arrangements to meet the following day. I telephoned Doris to advise her of the progress of the investigation. I asked her to tell no one of the status of the inquiry for fear the news might reach Jim and lessen the significance of his polygraph examination. She agreed.

THE FOLLOW-UP PHASE

The next day, Jim underwent the examination at my office. The results indicated deception when he denied participating in the theft of the checks. After reviewing the results of the examination with him and encouraging him to explain his involvement, Jim confessed that he had found the checks in the trash and had removed them from the bank. He had discussed the checks with his brother, Gaul, and then had asked JC to cash them in Las Vegas. Jim declared that JC had given him $700 in cash from the checks when he returned from Las Vegas. Jim signed a hand-written statement acknowledging his part in the theft of the checks, and he professed his willingness to repay the bank for the loss.

In Doris' office at the bank, I told her the outcome of the investigation. She told me that Jim had shown up for work as usual at 4:30. He willingly gave up his key to the bank and understood that he and his cleaning crew were not to return to the bank again. There still remained the matter of restitution. Doris told me that the bank would consider prosecution if Jim did not repay the money. Four days later, Jim and I met to talk over the repayment. Almost immediately, he said, "I didn't tell you the complete truth the other day. I got those checks from my brother, who had stolen them from the bank one Saturday about two weeks before I gave them to JC. Gaul had had them for a while before he told me about them, and I couldn't return them to the bank, so Gaul suggested I talk to JC about cashing them for me. I gave JC money for his plane tickets, and he agreed to give me some money after the cashing the checks. JC claimed he had to leave a place real quick in Vegas and had left $800 worth of checks behind because some guy was chasing him. I'm surprised that JC used his real name on those checks. I had told him that if the heat got too great, to say that he got the checks from me. I'm glad to hear that JC cashed all of the checks. Now I'll try to get some money from JC to offset my loss."

"You are willing to pay the bank for their cost in this matter, aren't you? You know the bank not only lost the checks, but they are spending a lot of money for my service to get this cleared up!"

"I know I've caused the bank trouble, and I want to make it right with them. I want to cover the checks and the cost of the investigation. I know your time doesn't come cheap! What do you think the whole thing will cost?"

"Well, the checks alone are $2,500," I said, and I told him what I thought my time would cost.

"Well then, I want to take care of it right and not have to owe the bank anything!"

"I suggest that you get a cashier's check for what you want to repay the bank and give it to them, or give it to me to give to them. Be sure it's made out in the name of the bank so everything is properly handled."

"I have something I can sell or get a loan on to get the money, so I won't have any trouble getting it!" he said.

After talking with Jim, I phoned Doris and told her what I had learned. It was now a wait-and-see situation. Doris declared that Jim had two weeks to repay the theft. "Prosecution is still a pending matter," she said. I advised Jim by phone of the bank's position and the two-week deadline. Jim said he hoped he could come up with the money within the next two weeks.

Thirteen days later, Jim phoned me to say that he would need another two weeks to come up with the repayment. He wanted me to ask the bank for an extension. I agreed to contact the bank on his behalf. Doris reluctantly agreed to allow Jim the extra two weeks. One week later, Jim told me that he had the money. He wanted me to take the cashier's check to the bank for him. I agreed. Jim provided a cashier's check drawn to the order of the bank. I took it to the bank with his apologies for causing so much trouble. The case had taken three months to this point.

About a year later, Jim telephoned me to ask if I could help him get the money from JC that he owed him from the cashed traveler's checks. Jim still thought JC was holding out on him. I did not see how I could help unless he sued JC and I testified about the details of the investigation. But did Jim really want that much publicity about his problem? He didn't!

Soli Deo Gloria

Bibliography

Abrams, Stanley, A. *Polygraph Handbook for Attorneys*. Lexington, MA: Lexington Books, 1977.

Adorno, T.W., Else Frenkel-Brunswik, Daniel F. Levinson, and R. Nevitt. *The Authoritarian Personality*. New York: Sanford, Harper and Brothers, 1950.

American Psychiatric Association (APA). *Diagnostic and Statistical Manual of Mental Disorders, 3rd ed*. Washington, DC: APA, 1980.

Attorney General Hubert H. Humphrey III, *Report on Scott County Investigations*, Feb. 12, 1985, p. 10. Library of Congress: HQ 72.U53 M64 1985, MN Attorney General, St. Paul, MN, 29 pages.

Aubry, Arthur S., Jr., and Rudolph R. Caputo. *Criminal Interrogation*. Springfield, IL: Charles C Thomas, 1980.

Banaka, William H. *Training in Depth Interviewing*. New York: Harper and Row, 1971.

Barbakow, Jeffrey C. Chief Executive (US). New York "The Ethics Patrol," July/August 1995, pp. 58-62.

Benjamin, Alfred. *The Helping Interview*. Boston: Houghton Mifflin, 1974.

Bennis, W.G., D.E. Berlew, E.H. Schein, and F.I. Steel, eds. *Interpersonal Dynamics: Essays and Readings on Human Interaction*. 3rd ed. Homewood, IL: Dorsey Press, 1973.

Berg, Irwin A., and Bernard M. Bass, eds. *Conformity and Deviation*. New York: Harper and Brothers, 1961.

Berne, Eric. *Games People Play*. New York: Grove, 1974.

———. *Intuition and Ego States*. San Francisco: TA Press, 1977.

Binder, D.A., and S.C. Price. *Legal Interviewing and Counseling*. St. Paul: West, 1977.

Birdwhistell, R.L. *Kinesics and Context: Essays on Body Communication*. Philadelphia: University of Pennsylvania Press, 1970.

Boorstin, Daniel. *The Image*. New York: Atheneum, 1972.

Bowers, David A. *Systems of Organization*. Ann Arbor: University of Michigan Press, 1976.

Brady, John. *The Craft of Interviewing*. New York: Vantage, 1977.

Bynum, W.F., E.J. Browne, and Roy Porter. *Dictionary of the History of Science*. Princeton, NJ: Princeton University Press, 1982.

Cameron, Norman, and Ann Margaret Cameron. *Behavior Pathology*. Boston: Riverside Press, 1951.

Cannon, W.B. *Bodily Changes in Pain, Horror, Fear and Rage*. New York: Appleton-Century-Crofts, 1929.

Cavanagh, Michael E. *How to Handle Your Anger*. 4th ed. Washington, DC: U.S. Dept. of Labor, Employment and Training Administration, 1979.

Cleckley, Hervey M. *The Mask of Sanity: An Attempt to Clarify Some Issues about the So-called Sociopathic Personality*. 5th ed. St. Louis: Mosby, 1976.

Cocke, E.W., Dr. "Constitutional Psychopathic Personality in Relation to Present-Day Crime and Delinquency" *The Peace Officer*, Vol. X, No. 1, 1953, p. 13.

Coleman, James C. *Abnormal Psychology and Modern Life*. 5th ed. Glenview, IL: Scott, Foresman, 1976.

Communication: The Non-Verbal Agenda. Film. New York: McGraw-Hill Films, 1975.

Davis, Flora. *Inside Intuition*. New York: New American Library, Times Mirror, 1975.

Dello, E.L. *Methods of Science*. New York: Universe Books, 1970.

Dewey, John. *Human Nature and Conduct*. New York: Modern Library, 1957.

Dexter, Lewis Anthony. *Elite and Specialized Interviewing*. Evanston, IL: Northwestern University Press, 1970.

Dougherty, George S. *The Criminal as a Human Being*. New York: Appleton, 1924.

Downs, Cal W., G. Paul Smeyak, and Ernest Martin. *Professional Interviewing*. New York: Harper and Row, 1980.

Drake, John D. *Interviewing for Managers: Sizing up People*. New York: American Management Association, 1972.

Eden, D., and J. Kinnar. "Modeling Galatea: Boosting Self-efficacy to Increase Volunteering." *Journal of Applied Psychology* 76/6 (Dec. 1991): 770–80.

The Effective Uses of Power and Authority. Film. New York: McGraw-Hill Films, 1980.

Egler, Frank E. *The Way of Science*. New York: Hafner, 1970.

Empathy in Police Work. Film. Madison, CT: L. Craig, Jr., producer, 1972.

The Empowerment Series. Videotape. Carlsbad, CA: CRM Films, 1992.

Fischer, Frank E. "A New Look at Management Communications." *Personnel* 31/6 (May 1955): 487-495.

Freeman, G.L., E.T. Katzoff, G.E. Manson, and J.H. Pathman. "The Stress Interview." *Journal of Abnormal and Social Psychology* 37 (1942): 427-447.

Freeman, H., and H. Weihofen. *Clinical Law Training: Interviewing and Counseling*. St. Paul: West, 1972.

Freud, Sigmund. *An Outline of Psycho-Analysis*. Translation by James Strachey. New York: W.W. Norton and Company, Inc., 1969.

Garrett, Annette. *Interviewing: Its Principles and Methods*. New York: Family Service Association of America, 1972.

Gist, M.E. "Self-efficacy: Implications for Organizational Behavior and Human Resource Management." *Academy of Management Review* 12/3 (1987): 472–85.

Gorden, Raymond L. *Interviewing Strategy, Techniques, and Tactics*. Homewood, IL: Dorsey Press, 1969.

Gunn, Battiscombe. *The Instruction of PTAH-HOTEP and the Instruction of KE'GEMNI: The Oldest Books in the World*. West London: John Murray, 1918.

Hall, E.T. *The Hidden Dimension*. New York: Doubleday, 1966.

Hare, Robert D. Dr. *Without Conscience*. Simon and Schuster, Inc., Pocket Books, New York, 1993.

Harre, Ron, and Roger Lamb, eds. *The Encyclopedic Dictionary of Psychology*. Cambridge, MA: MIT Press, 1983.

Harris, Thomas A. Videotape. *I'm Okay—You're Okay: A Practical Guide to Transactional Analysis*. Distributed by Success Motivation Institute, New York, by special arrangement with R.M. Karen and Harper and Row, 1973.

Hess, Karen M., and Henry M. Wrobleski. *For the Record: Report Writing in Law Enforcement*. Eureka, CA: Innovative Systems, 1988.

Hoffman, W. Michael and Edward S. Petry, Jr. "Abusing Business Ethics," *National Forum: Phi Kappa Phi Journal*. (Winter 1992), 72/1, p. 10-14.

Inbau, Fred, John Reid, and Joseph Buckley. *Criminal Interrogation and Confessions*. 3rd ed. Baltimore: Williams and Wilkins, 1986.

I Understand. You Understand. Film. Des Moines: Creative Media, 1975.

Kahn, Robert L., and Charles F. Cannell. *The Dynamics of Interviewing: Theory, Technique, and Cases*. New York: Wiley, 1957.

Karp, H.B., and Bob Abramms. "Doing the Right Thing." *Training and Development* 46/8 (August 1992). pp. 36-41.

Keefe, William F. *Listen Management*. New York: McGraw-Hill, 1971.

Kellihan, S.J. "Searching for the Meaning of the Truth and the Ethic of Its Use." Speech presented at the annual seminar of the American Polygraph Association, Vancouver, Canada, August 1982.

Kleinmuntz, Benjamin. *Essentials of Abnormal Psychology*. New York: Harper and Row, 1974.

Knapp, Mark. *Non-verbal Communication*. New York: Holt, Rinehart and Winston, 1972.

Kubler-Ross, Elizabeth. *On Death and Dying*. New York: Macmillan, 1969.

Levere, Trevor H. "Science." *Collier's Encyclopedia*, vol. 20. New York: Macmillan, l995, pp. 498A-499.

Lopez, Felix. *Personnel Interviewing*. New York: McGraw-Hill, 1975.

Mallory, James D., Jr. *The Kink and I*. Wheaton, IL: Victor, 1977.

Maltz, Maxwell. *Psycho-cybernetics*. Englewood Cliffs, NJ: Prentice-Hall, 1960.

Maslow, Abraham H. *Motivation and Personality*. New York: Harper, 1954.

Matson, Jack V. *Effective Expert Witnessing*. Chelsea, MI: Lewis Publishers, Inc., 1990.

McClelland, David. *Motivational Management*. Boston: Forum Corporation of North America, 1976.

McCormick, Charles T. *Evidence*. Hornbook Series. St. Paul: West, 1954.

McGregor, Douglas Murray. *The Human Side of Enterprise*. New York: McGraw-Hill, 1960.

Menninger, William C. *What Makes an Effective Man*. Personnel Series no. 152. New York: American Management Association, 1953.

Minnesota Crime Information 1994, prepared by: Minnesota Dept. of Public Safety, Bureau of Criminal Apprehension, St. Paul, MN, 55104

Minnick, Wayne C. *The Art of Persuasion*. Boston: Houghton Mifflin, 1985.

Nierenberg, Gerard I. *The Art of Negotiating*. New York: Cornerstone, 1968.

Nirenberg, Jesse S. *Getting through to People*. Englewood Cliffs, NJ: Prentice-Hall, 1963.

Nonverbal Communication. Film. New York: Harper and Row, 1976.

Office of Strategic Services (OSS) Assessment Staff. *Assessment of Men: Selection of Personnel for the Office of Strategic Services*. New York: Rinehart, 1948.

Officer Stress Awareness. Film. New York: Harper and Row, 1976.

Petry, Edward S., Jr. "Can Ethics Officers Improve Office Ethics?" *Business Society Review*, (Summer 1992) issue #82, pp. 21-25.

Phillips, D.L., and K. Clancy. "Modeling Effects in Survey Research." *Public Opinion Quarterly* 36/2 (Summer 1972): 246-253.

Productivity and the Self-Fulfilling Prophecy: The Pygmalion Effect. Film. New York: McGraw-Hill Films, 1975

Quinn, L., and N. Zunin. *Contact: The First Four Minutes*. Los Angeles: Nash, 1972.

Reusch, Jurgen, and Weldon Kees. *Nonverbal Communication*. Berkeley: University of California Press, 1954.

Rogers, Carl R. *Counseling and Psychotherapy*. Boston: Houghton Mifflin, 1942.

Ross, Alec, and David Plant. *Writing Police Reports: A Practical Guide*. Schiller Park, IL: Motorola Teleprograms, 1979.

Royal, Robert F., and Steven R. Schutt. *The Gentle Art of Interviewing and Interrogation*. Englewood Cliffs, NJ: Prentice-Hall, 1976.

Sapir, Edward. *Selected Writings of Edward Sapir*. D. G. Mandelbaum, ed. Berkeley and Los Angeles: University of California Press, 1949.

Scheflen, A.E. "Significance of Posture in Communications Systems." *Psychiatry* 27/4 (November 1964): pp. 316-331.

Schultz, William C. *The Interpersonal Underworld*. Palo Alto, CA: Science and Behavior Books, 1966.

Bridgeman, Percy W. and Gerald Holton. "Scientific Methods." *McGraw-Hill Encyclopedia of Science and Technology*. 5th ed. New York: McGraw-Hill, 1982.

Selling to Touch Customers. Film. Del Mar, CA: McGraw-Hill Films, 1981.

Selye, Hans. *Stress without Distress*. New York: American Library. 1975.

Shaw, George Bernard. *Pygmalion*. Dover Publications, Mineola, New York, 1994. (Originally published 1912).

Sherwood, Hugh. *The Journalistic Interview*. New York: Harper and Row, 1972.

Simons, Hebert W. *Persuasion*. Reading, MA: Addison-Wesley, 1976.

Sipe, H. Craig. "Science." *World Book Encyclopedia*, vol. 17. Chicago, IL: World Book, Inc., 1985.

Social Security Administration. *Interviewing and Counseling*. Washington, DC: U.S. Dept. of Health, Education and Welfare, Social Security Administration, 1964.

Stewart, Charles J., and William B. Cash. *Interviewing*. Dubuque, IA: William C. Brown, 1978.

———. *Interviewing: Principles and Practices*. Dubuque, IA: William C. Brown, 1974.

Thompson, George N. *The Psychopathic Delinquent and Criminal.* Springfield, IL: Charles C Thomas, 1953), p. 42.

Toffler, Alvin. *Future Shock.* New York: Random House, 1970.

Uniform Crime Reports for the United States, 1994, release date: November 19, 1995, printed annually by the Federal Bureau of Investigation, U.S. Department of Justice, Washington, D.C. 20535.

Wenger, M. A., Jones, F. N., and Jones, M. H. *Physiological Psychology.* New York: Henry Holt, 1956.

White, J. *The Autonomic Nervous System.* New York: MacMillan, 1952.

Wicks, Robert J., and Ernest H. Josephs, Jr. *Techniques in Interviewing for Law Enforcement and Corrections Personnel.* Springfield, IL: Charles C Thomas, 1972.

Wiley, Carolyn. "The ABCs of Business Ethics: Definition, Philosophies and Implementation." *Industrial Management.* (Jan./Feb. 1995) 37/1, pp. 22–26.

Woody, Robert J. and Woody, Jane D., eds. *Clinical Assessment in Counseling and Psychotherapy.* New York: Appleton, Century, Crofts, Meredith, 1972.

Yeschke, Charles L. "The Advantages and Limitations of Police Applicant Testing with the Polygraph." Paper presented at the ninth annual meeting of the American Academy of Polygraph Examiners, Chicago, Illinois, Aug. 1962.

———. "Banking on Police and Polygraphy." *Commercial West* 173/36 (Sept. 3, 1988): 14–15.

———. "A Bargain for Life: Basics of Hostage Negotiations." *Ohio Police* (Dec. 1981): 23–39.

———. "Coping with the Artful Dodgers: A Guide for the Polygraph Investigator." *Minnesota Police Chief* 2/3 (Summer1982): 49–55.

———. "The Cost of Interviewing." *American Society for Industrial Security, Central Minnesota Chapter Newsletter—Tell It A.S.I.S.* Minneapolis MN, 2/1 (Jan./Feb. 1984): 1–4.

———. "Effective Interviewing: A Skill No Officer Can Afford to Be Without." *Police Benevolent Association Journal* 7/2 (Winter 1982): 11–15.

———. "Ethical Considerations for Polygraph Examiners." Paper presented at the tenth annual meeting of the American Academy of Polygraph Examiners, Chicago, Illinois, Sept. 1963.

————. "Ethics and the Polygraph Examiner." *Journal of Criminal Law. Criminology and Police Science* 56/1 (Mar. 1965): 109–112.

————. "Fraud/Embezzlement: What to Do?" Unpublished paper presented during conference of Independent Bankers of Minnesota, Bloomington, MN, Fall 1989.

————. "Innocence, Bravery and Reality: A Tribute to John Scanlon." *Minnesota Police Chief* 5/3 (Sept. 1985): 47–49.

————. *Interviewing: A Forensic Guide to Interrogation.* 2nd ed. Springfield, IL: Charles C Thomas, 1993.

————. *Interviewing: An Introduction to Interrogation.* Springfield, IL: Charles C Thomas, 1987.

————. "Interviewing Door-to-Door: In Search of the Elusive." *Illinois Police Officer* 16/3 (Autumn 1985): 149–55.

————. "Local Police and Polygraphy." *Minnesota Police Chief* 9/1 (Mar. 1989): 123–33.

————. "Nice Guys Make Better Interviewers." *Law and Order* 30/8 (Aug. 1982): 67–69.

————. "The Polygraph Dodger." *Minnesota Sheriff* 20/3 (Summer 1982): 23–27.

————. "Polygraphy: A Unique Profession." *Minnesota Freelancer* (quarterly publication of the Minnesota Freelance Court Reporters Association) 1/2 (Fall 1985): 26–28.

————. "Positive Use of Power in Police Interviewing/Interrogating." *Law and Order* 31/9 (1983): 67–70.

————. "What to Do When Bank Managers Suspect Employees of Embezzlement." *Commercial West* (Oct. 9, 1982): 12–33.

————. "Why You Shouldn't Forget about That $1200 Embezzlement." *Commercial West* (Jan. 24, 1981): 12–13.

————. "Written Security Policies Can Stem Theft by Bank Employees." *Commercial West* (June 26, 1982): 20–33.

Zuckerman, Harriet. *Scientific Elite.* London: Free Press, Collier Macmillan, 1977.

Index